D0764763

designer
smocking
for tots to teens

First published in North America by

700 East State Street • Iola, WI 54990-0001
715-445-2214 • 888-457-2873
www.krausebooks.com

First published in Australia in 2007 by
COUNTRY BUMPKIN PUBLICATIONS
315 UNLEY RD, MALVERN, SOUTH AUSTRALIA 5061
www.countrybumpkin.com.au
Copyright© Country Bumpkin Publications 2007

ISBN-13: 978-0-89689-646-8
ISBN-10: 0-89689-646-3

EDITOR
Helen Davies

ASSISTANT EDITOR
Kathleen Barac

EDITORIAL ASSISTANTS
Marian Carpenter, Lizzie Kulinski
Heidi Reid, Joy Peters

GRAPHIC DESIGNER
Ann Jefferies

PATTERN DESIGNER & ILLUSTRATIONS
Kathleen Barac

STYLIST
Elizabeth Peterson

PHOTOGRAPHY
Andrew Dunbar Photography

PUBLISHER
Margie Bauer

PRINTED IN CHINA

Our toll-free number to place an order or
obtain a free catalog is (800) 258-0929

Welcome

'A child with a sense of style - has an awareness of self'

A sense of fashion can start at a very early age. Just ask the frustrated parent who has tried to change the mind of a child determined to wear a cherished piece of clothing. Choosing what to wear is often one of the first ways a child expresses their own distinct individuality.

This innovative collection of contemporary clothing and stylish accessories has been designed with a modern slant on an old favorite…smocking. However, the styling here is far removed from the familiar, almost formal appearance of traditional smocking. Whether they're enjoying an outdoor adventure or simply chilling out, your children will love to wear these outfits…and their friends are sure to be impressed.

Easy care fabrics in girlie prints, funky stripes, cool whites, earth tones and bold colors were used to create the garments, making them versatile enough for everyday wear and beyond. The sizes range from babies to early teens and every little body in between. Junior boys haven't been forgotten, as we show you how to add a touch of originality to their favorite denim shorts or jeans. The creative trimmings could just as easily be added to a jacket, shirt or T-shirt.

The designs vary from super easy which are perfect for beginners, to more advanced techniques which will extend your skills. By using our full-size patterns and detailed step-by-step instructions, with love and care, anyone can create a wardrobe of unique clothing for a special child, ensuring each item is made to last.

Contents

The ideal outfit for a stroll
on a hot summer's day

Golden Sands

By **Elizabeth Peterson**

School's out and the beach beckons! Sure to be a hit with pre-teens, this outfit has a stylish white knit top, with amber pebble beads decorating the smocking, and a hip hugging smocked skirt in earthy tones.

Requirements for top

Sizes 8, 10, 12 and 14 years

Fabric

White cotton lightweight rugby knit 59" (150cm) wide
Sizes 8 and 10: 20" (50cm)
Sizes 12 and 14: 24" (60cm)

Notions

43 ¼" x ³⁄₁₆" wide (1.1m x 4mm) white elastic
Fine tip water-soluble fabric marker
No. 7 crewel needle (smocking & embroidery)

Threads and beads

See page 12.

Requirements for skirt

Sizes 8, 10, 12 and 14 years

Fabric

Latté lightweight polycotton gabardine
59" (150cm) wide
Sizes 8 and 10: 59" (1.5m)
Sizes 12 and 14: 63" (1.6m)

Notions

8" (20cm) beige invisible zipper
Hook and eye
No. 7 crewel needle (smocking)
No. 12 (1.00mm) crochet hook

Threads

See page 12.

Pattern

See the liftout pattern sheet.

We recommend that you read the complete article and the liftout pattern instructions relating to this project before you begin.

The finished back length of the top from the shoulder to the hemline is
Size 8: 16 ⅛" (41cm)
Size 10: 17 ¼" (44cm)
Size 12: 18 ½" (47cm)
Size 14: 19 ¾" (50cm)

The finished back length of the skirt is

Size 8: 22" (56cm)

Size 10: 23 ⅝" (60cm)

Size 12: 25 ¼" (64cm)

Size 14: 26 ¾" (68cm)

There is no hem allowance on either garment.

Cutting Out

See the liftout pattern sheet for the cutting layouts and armhole template.

Top

White cotton rugby knit

Front: cut one

Size 8: 14 ⅛" x 27 ½" wide (36cm x 70cm)

Size 10: 15" x 27 ½" wide (38cm x 70cm)

Size 12: 15 ¾" x 29 ½" wide (40cm x 75cm)

Size 14: 16 ½" x 29 ½" wide (42cm x 75cm)

Using the armhole template and the fabric marker, mark the armhole shaping in both upper corners on the wrong side of the fabric. Mark a point ¾" (2cm) up from the lower edge at the center front. Rule a straight line 2" (5cm) out from this point and then taper it to the sides *(diag 1)*.

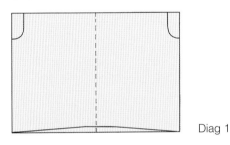

Diag 1

Note: the armholes and lower edge shaping will be cut out when the smocking is complete.

Skirt

Latté lightweight polycotton gabardine

Front and back skirt: cut two, each

Size 8: 20 ½" x 49 ¼" wide (52cm x 125cm)

Size 10: 22 ¼" x 49 ¼" wide (56.5cm x 125cm)

Size 12: 23 ⅝" x 59" wide (60cm x 150cm)

Size 14: 25" x 59" wide (63.5cm x 150cm)

Trace the pattern pieces onto lightweight interfacing or tracing paper, transferring the pattern markings. Cut out the remaining pieces for the top and skirt following the instructions on the pattern sheet.

Preparation & Pleating

Top

Pleat 11 full space rows (including two holding rows) with the top row ³⁄₁₆" (5mm) from the upper raw edge.

Unpick the pleating threads up to the marked armhole shaping, leaving ⅜" (1cm) for the seam allowance at each side *(diag 2)*.

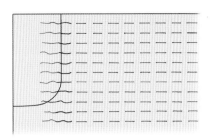

Diag 2

Tie off to fit the front blocking guide.

Skirt

Front and back

Pleat 8 full space rows (including two holding rows) with the top holding row ³⁄₁₆" (5mm) from the upper raw edge on each rectangle cut for the skirt.

Unpick the pleating threads for ⅝" (1.5cm) on each side for the seam allowance. Tie off each piece to fit the width of the corresponding yoke at the lower edge.

Smocking

See the step-by-step instructions for cable stitch on page 80, double cable on page 81 and full space wave on page 84.

Refer to the graph on page 11 and color key on page 12 for thread color and number of strands used.

Top

Count the pleats and mark the center valley.

Row 1 - 2. Beginning at the center two pleats on row 1 with an over cable, wave down to row 2, under cable, wave up to row 1. Continue to the end of the row. Turn the work upside down, return to the center and complete the row.

Row 1. Beginning at the center two pleats just above row 1 with an under cable, work cable stitch to the end of the row. Turn the work upside down, return to the center and complete the row.

Rows 2 - 5. Repeat row 1 - 2 three times.

Rows 5 - 9. Beginning with an over cable on the center two pleats, work eleven full space waves between rows 5 and 6 ending with an over cable on row 5. Turn the work upside down, return to the center and stitch another eleven full space waves to complete the row. Stitch three more rows of full space wave in a similar manner, omitting three waves at the end of each row.

Hint

The crocheted edge is best worked along the tuck and hem after the skirt is constructed.

Skirt

Smock the design on both skirt pieces in the same manner. All rows are worked from left to right.

Row 1. Double cable. Beginning with an over cable, work a row of cable stitch along row 1. Work a mirror image cable row just below the first.

Rows 2, 5 and 6. Repeat the previous two rows, placing the rows of cable following the graph.

Row 2 - 5. Wave stitch. Beginning with an over cable just below the cables on row 2, wave down to just above row 5, under cable, wave up to row 2. Continue across the row, keeping the tension even and taking care not to pull the long stitches too tight.

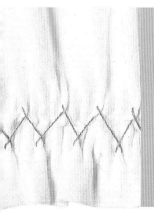

Hint

After constructing the top, use the lines of machine stitching as a guide to place the herringbone stitches and take care not to make the stitching too tight.

Backsmocking

Work rows of cable stitch along rows 3 and 4.

Embroidery

See page 12 for the embroidery key.
See the step-by-step instructions for herringbone stitch on page 13.

Top

Construct the top following the instructions on pages 94 and 95.

Beading

Using A, attach a small stone chip bead on the center two pleats of the last row of wave stitch at the position marked on the graph. Secure five larger beads radiating around the center bead to form a flower. Stitch a single bead over the second under cable on both ends of the incomplete rows of wave stitch.

Embroidery

Work herringbone stitch between the two rows of elastic at the lower edge of the top, taking each stitch through a fold in the fabric formed by the casing. Take care not to pull the stitches too tight between the rows.

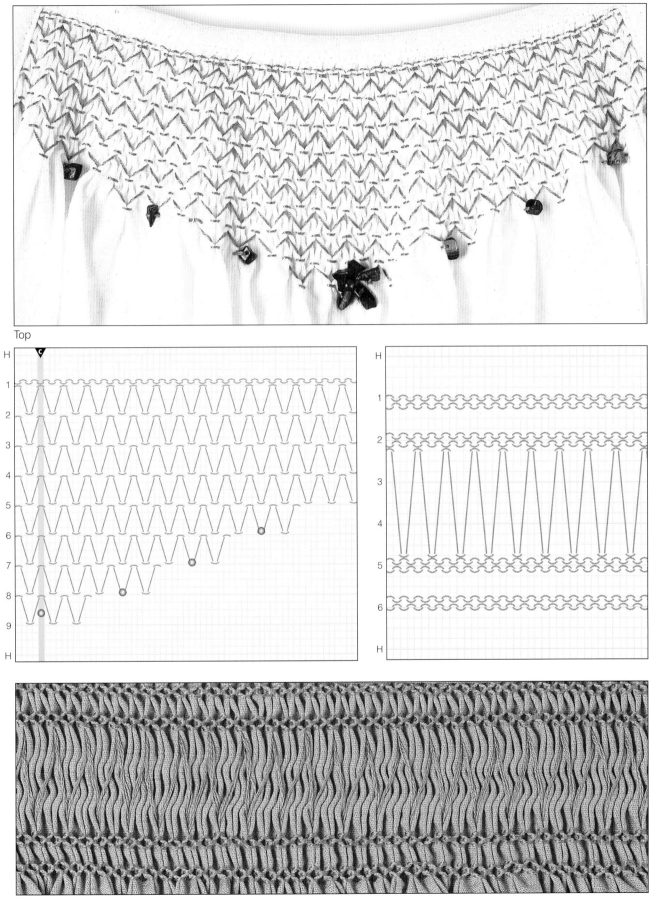

Top

Skirt

Skirt

Construct the skirt following the instructions on pages 95 and 96.

Crocheted edge

Using 1 strand of C and the crochet hook, work the edging along the fold of each tuck and the hem.

With the right side facing, begin close to one side seam (but not directly on the seam). Push the crochet hook through both layers of the fold, approximately ⅛" (2mm) from the edge. Catch the thread 6" (15cm) from the end and draw a loop through the fabric (diag 3).

Diag 3

Complete the slip stitch by catching the working thread and drawing a loop through the first loop (diag 4).

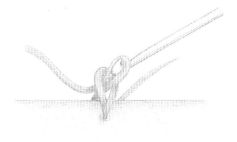

Diag 4

Work three more chain stitches in the same manner (diag 5).

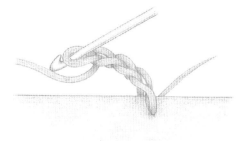

Diag 5

Push the crochet hook through the fold approximately ⅜" (1cm) away from the first slip stitch and draw a loop through the fabric. Work a slip stitch by pulling the loop through the first loop on the hook (diag 6).

Diag 6

Continue to work three chains, 1 loop through the fold (at ⅜" (1cm) intervals), 1 slip stitch, in the same manner along the edge of the tuck (diag 7).

Diag 7

At the beginning, work a slip stitch through the first slip stitch (diag 8).

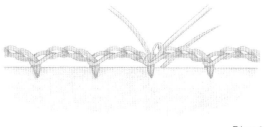

Diag 8

Cut the thread and pull the tail through the loop just formed. End off by weaving this tail and the one at the beginning through the crocheted edge.

Construction

See pages 94 - 96.

Color Key

Top

DMC stranded cotton
A = 841 lt beige
Stone chip beads
B = amber

Skirt

DMC no. 8 perlé cotton
C = 841 lt beige (2 balls)

Smocking = A (3 strands)
Embroidery = A (3 strands)
Beading = A & B (1 strand)
Crochet edge = C (1 strand)

Embroidery Key

Herringbone stitch = A (3 strands)

Herringbone Stitch

The elastic casing on the lower edge of the top has been decorated by adding the textural contrast of herringbone stitch over the folds in the fabric.

Use the lines of machine stitching securing the elastic as a guide for the upper and lower placement of the stitches. The pencil lines in the photos represent the rows of stitching.

It is not necessary to stretch the elastic while you stitch.

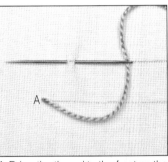

1. Bring the thread to the front on the left hand side of a fold in the fabric on the lower level (A). With the thread below the needle, take a stitch from right to left through a fold on the upper row of stitching approx ¼" (6mm) to the right of A.

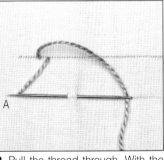

2. Pull the thread through. With the thread above the needle, take a stitch from right to left through a fold on the lower row of stitching approx ⅜" - ½" (10 - 13mm) to the right of A.

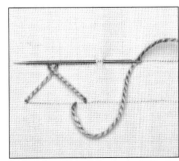

3. Pull the thread through. With the thread below the needle, take a stitch on the upper row as before (the same distance away).

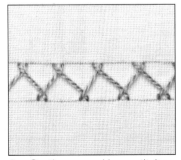

4. Continue working stitches, alternating between the upper and lower rows.

For work or play, durable denim is always in style

Little worker

By **Kathleen Barac**

Embellish a pair of denim shorts for your junior construction engineer with this set of picture smocked patches. Other trims include decorative stitching, a purchased embroidered motif, plus tabs and loops made from striped grosgrain ribbon. The designs and ideas shown here can also be used to embellish other items of clothing.

Requirements

Fabric
Khaki cotton homespun, poplin or similar strong, lightweight fabric for the inserts
10" x 44" wide (25cm x 112cm)

Notions
15 ¾" x ¾" wide (40cm x 20mm) striped grosgrain ribbon
4 x 1" (25mm) wide silver 'D' rings
1 x embroidered motif to suit the theme
2.5/80 sewing machine twin needle
Red machine topstitching thread
Water-soluble fabric marker
No. 7 crewel needle (smocking)
No. 8 milliner's needle (embroidery)

Threads
See pages 18 and 19.

Cutting out
We recommend that you read the complete article and the instructions relating to this project before you begin.

Inserts
Workman: cut one,
5 ½" x 19 ¾" wide (14cm x 50cm)
Hammer and drill: cut two, each
4" x 19 ¾" wide (10cm x 50cm)

Linings
Workman: cut one,
4 ½" x 4 ¾" wide (11.5cm x 12cm)
Hammer and drill: cut two, each
3 ½" x 4 ⅛" wide (9cm x 10.5cm)
The finished size (to the topstitched border) of each patch is
Workman: 3 ⅜" x 3 ⅝" wide (8.5cm x 9cm)
Hammer and drill: 2 ⅜" x 3" wide (6cm x 7.5cm)

Pleating

Workman

Pleat 12 full space rows with the first row ⅝" (1.5cm) from the upper raw edge.

Unpick the pleating threads for ⅝" (1.5cm) at one side of the panel. Count 62 pleats and unpick the remaining pleats. Trim off the extra fabric, leaving a ⅝" (1.5cm) seam allowance. Tie off so that the pleated area measures 3 ⅝" (9cm) wide.

Hammer and drill

For each piece, pleat 7 full space rows, with the first row ⅝" (1.5cm) from the upper raw edge.

Each panel contains 56 pleats. Unpick the pleating threads and prepare the panels in the same manner as before. Tie off so that the pleated area measures 3 ⅛" (8cm) wide.

Smocking

See pages 22-25 for the step-by-step instructions for working the picture smocked designs and page 91 for the outline stitch instructions.

Workman

Begin on the sixteenth pleat from the left of the panel on row 5 at the position marked on the graph. Stitch the main areas of the workman first, adding the hands and tools last. The shovel is worked from the cables forming the handle, then satin stitching down the shaft, ending with the light grey cables of the blade.

Hammer

Begin on the tenth pleat from the left of the panel just below row 4 at the position marked on the graph. Stitch the grey areas of the head and shaft first, then the diagonal stripes of the handle grip. Finally, work the light tan satin stitching at the base of the grip.

The multi-colored borders above and below the hammer consist of three outline stitch rows worked closely together. Using C, work the first row of outline stitch along row 2. Stitch a second row immediately above the first (using B) and another just below (using D). Stitch the lower border in a similar manner, with the first row along row 6 and reversing the colors of the other two rows.

Drill

Begin the body of the drill on the seventeenth pleat from the left of the panel on row 3 at the position marked on the graph. Add the drill bit, using stem stitch, after you have completed the stacked cables. Work the diagonal markings and outline the segments of the drill, referring to the graph and the photo for placement.

When the stacked cables are finished, there may be areas of a design where the unused pleats gape open beside straight edges of stitching. To correct this problem, handstitch the two pleats together on the wrong side using back stitch.

Place the stitching half way up the pleats and try not to tighten them as this will distort the pleats and the stitching on the right side *(diag 1).*

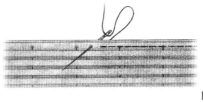

Diag 1

Backsmocking

On each patch, work a row of cable stitch along each pleating row.

Embroidery

See pages 18 and 19 for the embroidery keys.

These designs use outline stitch, stem stitch, chain stitch, satin stitch and straight stitch.

Work the detailing on the workman and the drill, referring to the close-up photos and the graphs for placement. Follow the embroidery keys for the colors and method of stitching.

Construction

See pages 20 and 21 for the step-by-step instructions for inserting the patches and adding the grosgrain tabs.

Hints on Picture Smocking

- Picture smocking is best worked on pleats that are close together but not quite touching.

- Stranded threads are most effective. Always strip the individual strands and reassemble them before starting. Four or five strands work well for most designs but if you are using light colored threads on dark fabric, you may need an extra strand or two to provide adequate coverage.

- The easiest place to begin a design is on a pleating row. Select one of the widest rows in the motif.

- The stitches should be placed ⅔ - ¾ of the way down from the top of the pleat. This will prevent the background fabric showing through the gaps between the stitches and will help to maintain sharp lines on the edges of the blocks of color.

- Keep your stitch tension even and slightly looser than geometric smocking. The pleats should remain straight and lie side by side. They should not be distorted or pulled together by the stitching.

- Use the pleating rows as a guide to keep the stitching straight, rather than the previous row of stitches.

The Workman

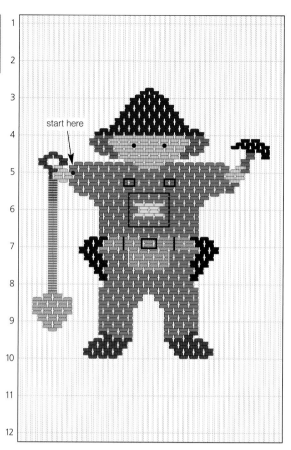

Color Key

DMC stranded cotton

A = 169 gun metal grey
B = 304 lt garnet
C = 434 brown
D = 535 lt charcoal
E = 798 dk delft
F = 987 forest green
G = 3064 med mocha

Anchor stranded cotton

H = 382 black-brown
I = 403 black
J = 874 lt mustard

Smocking = 4 strands (stacked cable and satin stitch)
Backsmocking = D (3 strands)

Smocking & Embroidery Key

All the smocking is worked with four strands unless otherwise specified.

Overalls

Pants, bib and straps = E (stacked cable)
Pocket badge = J (stacked cable)
Pocket outline = D (2 strands, back stitch)
Buckles = I (2 strands, straight stitch)
Hands and face = G (stacked cable)
Hair = C (stacked cable)
Eyes = I (French knot, 2 strands, 2 wraps)

Hard hat

Hat = B (stacked cable)
Insignia = A (straight stitch)

Tool belt

Belt and bag = A (stacked cable)
Tool holsters = I (stacked cable)
Belt loops = I (2 strands, bullion knot, 14 wraps)
Tool loops = D or I (2 strands, bullion loop, 24 wraps)
Buckle = I (2 strands, straight stitch)
Bag outline = D (2 strands, back stitch)
Boots = H (stacked cable)
Boot laces = C (2 strands, straight stitch)

Shovel

Handle = H (stacked cable)
Shaft = C and H (satin stitch)
Blade = A (stacked cable)

Hammer

Handle = C (stacked cable)
Head = I (stacked cable)

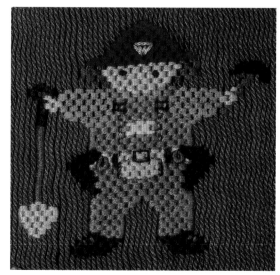

The Hammer

Color Key

DMC stranded cotton
A = 169 gun metal grey
B = 304 lt garnet
C = 434 lt brown
D = 535 lt charcoal
Anchor stranded cotton
E = 874 lt mustard
Smocking = 4 strands (stacked cable)
2 strands (outline stitch)
Backsmocking = D (3 strands)

Smocking & Embroidery Key

All the smocking is worked with four strands unless otherwise specified.
Head and shaft = A (stacked cable)
Handle grip = B and E (stacked cable)
Handle base = C (satin stitch)
Borders = B, C and D (outline stitch, 2 strands)

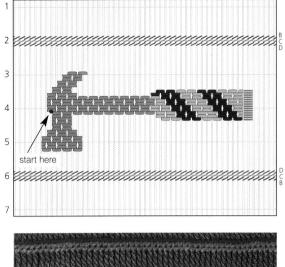

The Drill

Color Key

DMC stranded cotton
A = 434 lt brown
B = 648 lt beaver grey
C = 3022 med Jacobean green
D = 3768 dk grey-green
Anchor stranded cotton
E = 403 black
Rajmahal stranded rayon
F = 25 Lagerfeld ink
Smocking = 4 strands (stacked cable)
6 strands (stem stitch)
Backsmocking = E (3 strands)

Smocking & Embroidery Key

All the smocking is worked with four strands unless otherwise specified.
Drill = A, C, D and E (stacked cable)
Cord = E (stacked cable)
Drill bit = B (6 strands, stem stitch)
Outline = F (2 strands, chain stitch)
Markings = E (2 strands, straight stitch)

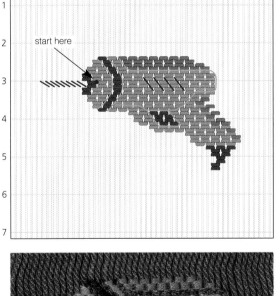

Inserting the patches

Note: the workman was placed into the left-hand back pocket because most boys are right handed and the pocket is not functional after the patch is inserted. Reverse the placement if your child is left handed.

The charm of this method of inserting the patches lies in its simplicity. Twin-needle stitching in contrasting sewing thread has been used but you may wish to experiment with other decorative stitches to attach the patches.

Cut the holes in the garment as close as possible to the straight grain of the fabric to keep the length of the fringing even.

The size of the outer rectangle marked in diagram 3 is

Workman
3 3/8" x 3 5/8" wide (8.5cm x 9cm)

Drill and hammer
2 3/8" x 3" wide (6cm x 7.5cm)

Insert the workman patch after attaching the 'D' ring strap closure above the pocket.

Block the patches to the original tied off measurement and leave to dry. With wrong sides together, pin the lining fabric behind the appropriate patch. Tack around the outer edges *(diag 1)*.

Diag 1

Machine baste, ensuring the pleats are straight and even. Trim and neaten the raw edges with an overlock or zigzag stitch *(diag 2)*.

Diag 2

Using the fabric marker and a ruler, measure and mark a rectangle in the chosen area of the garment. Mark a second rectangle 1/2" (13mm) inside the first *(diag 3)*.

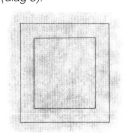

Diag 3

Cut out the inner rectangle and clip into the corners to within 1/8" (2 - 3mm) of the first marked line *(diag 4)*.

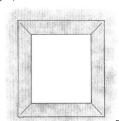

Diag 4

Center the patch behind the opening and pin in place. Tack close to the marked line *(diag 5)*.

Diag 5

Using the red machine thread in the twin-needle, stitch along the marked line through all layers *(diag 6)*. Raise the presser foot to pivot the fabric and reposition the stitching at each corner.

Diag 6

Remove the tacking. Using a pin or strong needle, remove the fabric threads that run parallel to the cut edges *(diag 7)*.

Diag 7

Fluff up the fringing with a stiff brush, holding a piece of cardboard under the fringe to protect the stitching on the patch. Finished patch *(diag 8)*.

Diag 8

Decorative Trims

Topstitching and faded effects on the shorts made it impractical to remove pockets or unpick seams in order to attach embellishments. The methods described here are simple but effective ways to trim a boy's purchased garment without having to dismantle it in the process.

Purchased motifs

As the pocket should remain functional, the patch should not be machine stitched in place. Pin or tack it in position. Then handstitch it to the pocket only, following the outer contours of the patch. Here, the simplest method was to use a row of backstitching (for strength), around the inner and outer circles. Another option could have been satin or buttonhole stitch in rayon thread to match the stitching around the outer rim of the patch.

'D' ring strap closure

The trim on the upper left pocket was machine stitched in place because the actual pocket inside the shorts could be held out of the way for both sections and wasn't secured by the stitching. This decorative closure could still be attached if there wasn't a second pocket above the lower one containing the workman patch.

Using a fabric marker, mark the center of the pocket on both edges of the opening.

Upper section

Cut a 3 ½" (9cm) piece of striped ribbon. Slip two 'D' rings onto the ribbon. Fold in half, bringing both raw ends to the center at the back and tack (fig 1). Pin in place, centered over the mark on the upper edge and with a ½" (13mm) loop extending below the fold containing the D rings.

fig 1

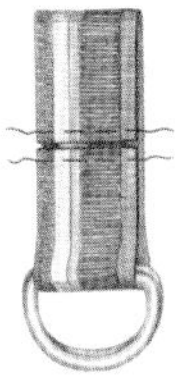

Stitch in place with a rectangle of red machine stitching, working around the rectangle twice (fig 2).

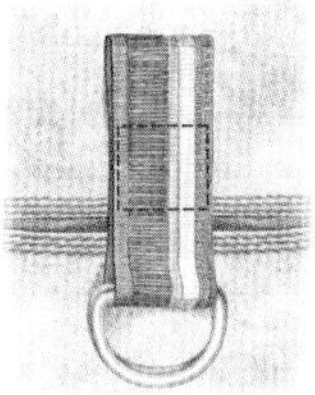

fig 2

Lower section

Cut an 7 ⅛" (18cm) piece of striped ribbon. Fold in half and stitch a 'V' in the folded end (fig 3).

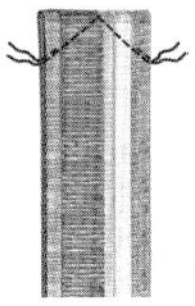

fig 3

Turn to the right side and push out the point. Topstitch down both sides and the pointed end using the red thread. Neaten the raw end with an overlock or zigzag stitch. Keeping the inside pocket out of the way, slip the strap inside the outer pocket, leaving 2 ⅜" (6cm) extending outside the pocket. Stitch up the sides of the lower end and across the ribbon just above the pocket edge (fig 4).

fig 4

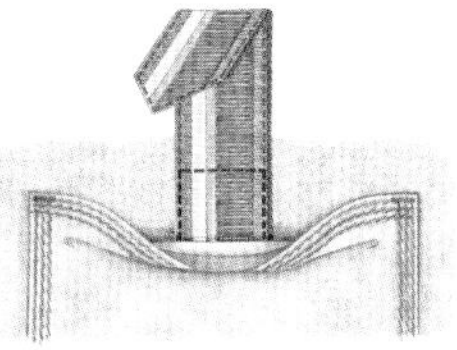

Pass the strap up through both 'D' rings and then back through the lower one, pulling to secure.

'D' ring loop

Cut a 2" (5cm) piece of striped ribbon. Slip on a 'D' ring. Fold in half and neaten the raw ends of the ribbon together with an overlock or zigzag stitch (fig 5).

Mark the center of the lower edge of the pocket. Mark slightly less than ⅜" (1cm) either side of the center. Using small pointed scissors, cut an opening in the fabric under the fold of the pocket between the two outer points.

fig 5

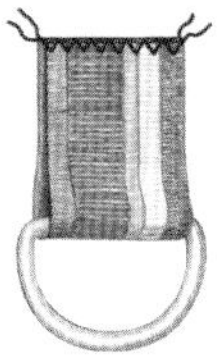

Slip the ribbon loop into the opening, leaving ⅜" (1cm) showing (fig 6).

On the wrong side, handstitch the ribbon to the fabric behind the pocket, including the raw edge of the opening (fig 7).

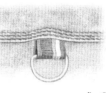
fig 6

Ensure this section is secure with several rows of tiny overcast stitches as it could fray in the wash and ruin the effect. On the right side handstitch the opening closed.

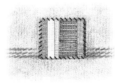
fig 7

Zigzag topstitching

Apart from being purely decorative, this stitching could also strengthen frayed and worn areas of a favorite pair of jeans. Using the straight stitch variation in the set of tricot (forward and reverse) stitches on your machine and the contrasting sewing thread, stitch over the desired area of your garment in a random zigzag pattern.

Picture smocking is also known as stacked cables. In this technique, multiple rows of cable stitch, worked in blocks of color, are stacked one upon the other to create figures, motifs and scenes. The stitches in one row are usually worked as a mirror image of the previous and subsequent rows, forming a brickwork pattern of cable stitches.

After the background areas are worked, a design is usually brought to life by outlining certain sections or by adding details using traditional embroidery stitches.

Because this form of smocking has very little elasticity, ensure the pleated fabric is close to the required finished width before you start smocking. Stretching the work afterwards to fit a blocking guide will distort the design.

Backsmocking is required to prevent the pleats from gaping in the unsmocked areas after the pleating threads are removed. This may be done before or after the picture smocking is worked.

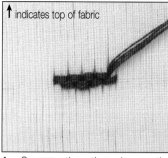

indicates top of fabric

1. Secure the thread on the back of the fabric. Beginning with an over cable, work cable across the row except for the last over cable.

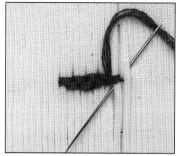

2. With the thread above and angling the needle, take it through the last two pleats and emerge a needle's width below the previous under cable.

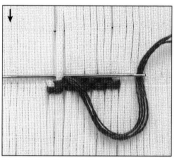

3. Pull the thread through. Turn the fabric upside down. Take the needle from right to left through the pleat to the left.

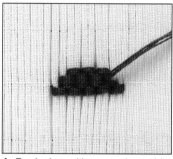

4. Beginning with an under cable, work cable across the row except for the last stitch.

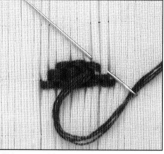

5. When working the last under cable, angle the needle back through two pleats, emerging a needle's width above the previous over cable.

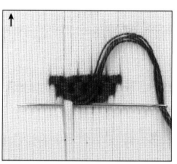

6. Turn the fabric up the right way. Take the needle from right to left through the pleat to the left.

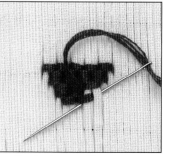

7. Beginning with an over cable, work cable across the row. Work the last over cable following step 2.

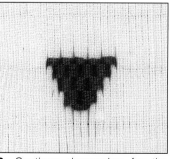

8. Continue decreasing for the required number of rows, turning the fabric after each row.

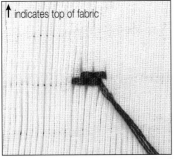

1. Secure the thread on the back of the fabric. Beginning with an under cable, work cable across the row except for the last under cable.

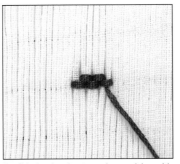

2. Stitch the last under cable with the thread above the needle so it will be in the correct position to start the next row.

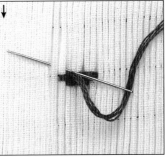

3. Turn the fabric. Keeping the thread below, angle the needle through the two pleats to the left two needles' width above the previous row.

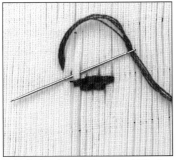

4. Pull the thread through. With the thread above and angling the needle, take it through the next pleat a needle's width above the previous row.

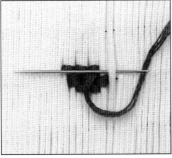

5. Pull the thread through. Continue in cable to the end of the row. Keep the thread below the needle for the last stitch (an over cable).

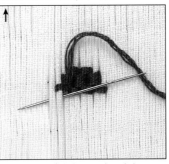

6. Turn the fabric up the right way. With thread above, angle the needle through the two pleats to the left, two needles' width below the previous row.

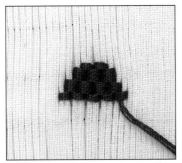

7. Beginning with an under cable, complete the row in the same manner as before.

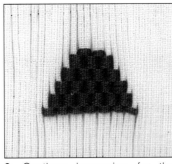

8. Continue increasing for the required number of rows, turning the fabric after each row.

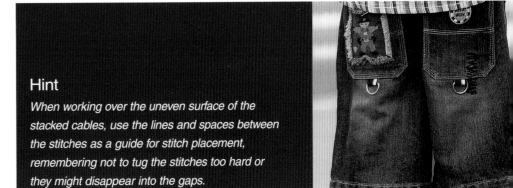

Hint

When working over the uneven surface of the stacked cables, use the lines and spaces between the stitches as a guide for stitch placement, remembering not to tug the stitches too hard or they might disappear into the gaps.

Picture Smocking - Straight Sides

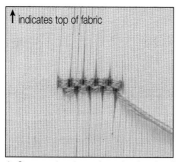

1. Secure the thread on the back of the fabric. Beginning and ending with an over cable, stitch across the row.

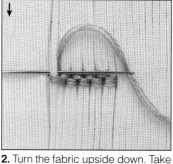

2. Turn the fabric upside down. Take the needle from right to left through the first pleat, just above the last cable stitch.

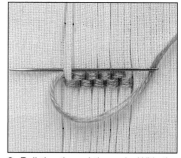

3. Pull the thread through. With the thread below, again take the needle from right to left through the same pleat a needle's width above the previous cable stitch.

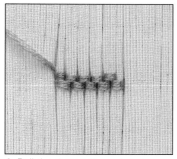

4. Pull the thread through to form a satin stitch over one pleat.

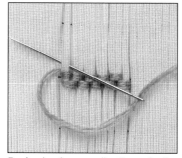

5. Angle the needle through the pleat, emerging a needle's width above the previous satin stitch.

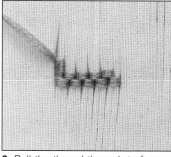

6. Pull the thread through to form a second satin stitch.

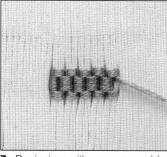

7. Beginning with an over cable, work a mirror image of the previous row of cables.

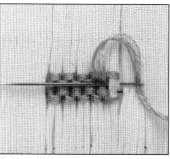

8. Keeping the thread above, take the needle from right to left through the last pleat, a needle's width below the last over cable (between the two rows).

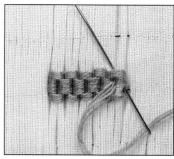

9. Pull the thread through. Take the needle from right to left through the same pleat, emerging above the over cable.

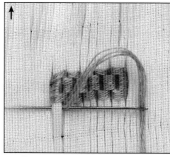

10. Pull the thread through. Turn the fabric up the right way. Take the needle through the first pleat, a needle's width below the previous cable stitch.

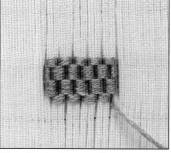

11. Beginning with an over cable, work a mirror image of the previous cable row.

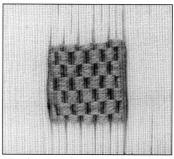

12. Continue working rows and adding satin stitches in the spaces formed.

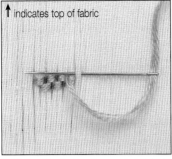

↑ indicates top of fabric

1. Using the first color, work cable to the color changeover point. Ensure the thread is below the needle for the last stitch - an over cable.

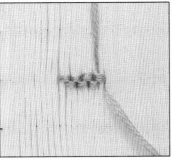

2. Secure the needle in the fabric and out of the way. Bring the second color to the front through the next valley.

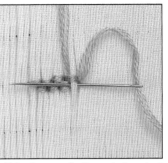

3. Take the needle through the pleat to the left just below the last stitch.

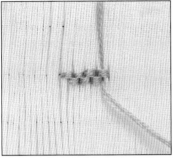

4. Pull the thread through ready to begin stitching.

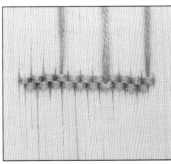

5. Beginning with an under cable, work cable to the next color changeover point. Ensure the thread is below for the last stitch - an under cable.

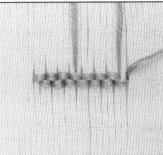

6. Secure the needle in the fabric and out of the way. Bring the third color to the front through the next valley.

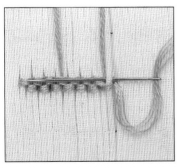

7. Take the needle through the pleat to the left just above the last stitch.

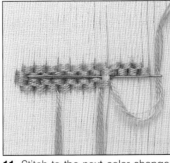

8. Pull the thread through. Beginning with an over cable, work cable to last stitch of third color. With thread below, work last stitch - an over cable.

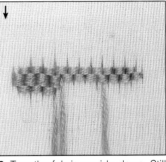

9. Turn the fabric upside down. Still using the third color and beginning and ending with an over cable, work to the color changeover point.

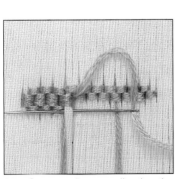

10. Secure the needle in the fabric and out of the way. Pick up the second color. Take the needle through the pleat to the left.

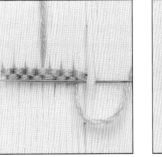

11. Stitch to the next color changeover point as before. Secure the needle in the fabric. Take the first color through the pleat to the left as before.

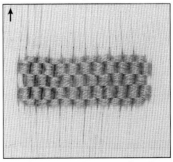

12. Complete the row. Continue working the required number of rows in the same manner, turning the fabric for each one.

In the jungle, the mighty jungle,
the lion sleeps tonight

Out of Africa

By **Elizabeth Peterson**

Ready for adventure, this practical military style dress features two panels of vertical smocking. Almost every seam and fold has been topstitched with thread to match the smocking.

Requirements

Sizes 6, 8 and 10 years

Fabric

Khaki lightweight polycotton gabardine
59" (150cm) wide
Size 6: 63" (1.6m)
Size 8: 67" (1.7m)
Size 10: 71" (1.8m)

Notions

16" x 20" wide (40cm x 50cm) piece of lightweight woven fusible interfacing
2" x 40" wide (5cm x 100cm) piece of heavyweight fusible interfacing
Machine topstitching thread to match the embroidery thread
10 x ⁵⁄₈" (18mm) bronze military style metal buttons
1 x 1 ¾" (4.5cm) wide bronze metal belt buckle
9 x ³⁄₈" (9mm) large bronze metal eyelets
No. 7 crewel needle (smocking)

Threads

See opposite page.

Pattern

See the liftout pattern sheet.

We recommend that you read the complete article and the liftout pattern instructions relating to this project before you begin.

The finished back length from the nape of the neck to the lower edge of the hem is
Size 6: 24 ¾" (63cm)
Size 8: 26 ¾" (68cm)
Size 10: 28 ¾" (73cm)
The hem allowance is 1 ¼" (3cm).

Cutting Out

See the liftout pattern sheet for the cutting layout.

Khaki lightweight polycotton gabardine

Left and right front inserts: cut two, each 4" (10cm) deep by the following measurement in width
Size 6: 43 ¼" (110cm)
Size 8: 45 ¼" (115cm)
Size 10: 47 ¼" (120cm)

Trace the pattern pieces onto lightweight interfacing or tracing paper, transferring the pattern markings. Cut out the remaining pieces following the instructions on the liftout pattern sheet.

Pleating

For each front insert, pleat 8 full space rows (including two holding rows), with the top holding row ⅝" (1.5cm) from the raw edge.

Unpick the pleating threads on both sides, leaving a ⅜" (1cm) seam allowance. Tie off so that the pleated area measures the following width

Size 6: 10 ⅝" (27cm)

Size 8: 11" (28cm)

Size 10: 11 ⅜" (29cm)

Smocking

See the step-by-step instructions for cable and alternating cable stitches on pages 80 and 82, and single feather stitch on page 83.

All rows, except the single feather stitch, can be worked from left to right.

Row 1. Cable. Beginning with an under cable, work a row of cable stitch along row 1.

Row 2. Alternating cable. Repeat the previous cable row along row 2. Stitch the cable picots above and below the cable row, beginning with three cables below.

Row 3. Repeat row 2, omitting the lower picots only.

Rows 4 - 6. Work a mirror image of rows 1 - 3.

Row 3 - 4. Referring to the graph for stitch placement and beginning just below the cables on row 3 on the right hand side of the panel, stitch a row of single feather stitch.

Construction

See pages 96 - 100.

Pocket

Color Key

DMC stranded cotton

A = 3021 vy dk Jacobean green (2 skeins)

Smocking = A (3 strands)

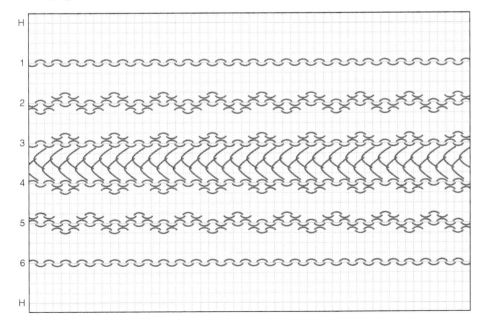

Insert

A cute summer outfit for
adventurous little girls

Flower Power

By **Angela Bostick**

Banish grey skies and winter blues with this delightful two-piece combination. A classic white top with embroidered straps and buttons is complemented by floral three-quarter pants. A charming beaded bracelet makes the perfect fashion accessory.

Requirements

Sizes 1, 2, 3 and 4 years

Top

Fabric

White polycotton poplin 44" (112cm) wide

Sizes 1 and 2: 43 ¼" (1.1m)

Sizes 3 and 4: 49 ¼" (1.25m)

Notions

12" x 20" wide (30cm x 50cm) piece of lightweight woven fusible interfacing

5 x ½" (12mm) four-hole white buttons

Fine tip water-soluble fabric marker

No. 7 crewel needle (smocking)

No. 8 milliner's needle (embroidery)

Capri pants

Fabric

Hot pink/mint cotton print 44" (112cm) wide

Sizes 1 and 2: 33 ½" (85cm)

Sizes 3 and 4: 39 ⅜" (1m)

Notions

20" x ¾" wide (51cm x 20mm) white non-roll elastic

Threads

See page 34.

Pattern

See the liftout pattern sheets.

We recommend that you read the complete article and the pattern instructions relating to this project before you begin.

The finished back length of the top from the shoulder to the hemline is

Size 1: 15" (38cm)

Size 2: 16 ½" (42cm)

Size 3: 18 ⅛" (46cm)

Size 4: 19 ¾" (50cm)

The finished side length of the pants is

Size 1: 15 ⅛" (38.5cm)

Size 2: 16 ½" (42cm)

Size 3: 17 ⅞" (45.5cm)

Size 4: 19 ¼" (49cm)

There is no hem allowance on either garment.

Cutting out

See the pattern sheet for the cutting layouts.

White polycotton poplin

Front: cut one

Size 1: 12 ¾" x 37 ½" wide (32.5cm x 95cm)

Size 2: 14" x 37 ½" wide (35.5cm x 95cm)

Size 3: 15 ¼" x 43 ¼" wide (38.5cm x 110cm)

Size 4: 16 ⅜" x 43 ¼" wide (41.5cm x 110cm)

Rectangle for straps: cut one

11 ¾" x 10" wide (30cm x 25cm)

The individual straps will be cut when the embroidery is complete.

Trace the pattern pieces onto lightweight interfacing or tracing paper, transferring the pattern markings. Cut out the remaining pieces following the instructions on the pattern sheet.

Preparation & Pleating

Beginning on the left, insert needles in the first six full space rows of the pleater. Leave five full spaces free and then insert needles in the next three full space rows. Using threads longer than the width of the fabric, pleat the front, placing the first row (in the group of three needles) ⅝" (1.5cm) from the upper raw edge *(diag 1)*.

Diag 1

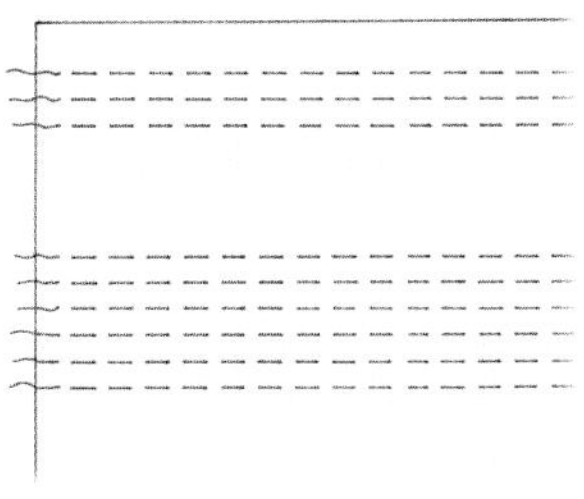

Unpick the pleating threads for ⅜" (1cm) at each side.

Flatten out the pleats. Fold under a narrow double hem on the upper raw edge and machine stitch close to the edge *(diag 2)*. Press.

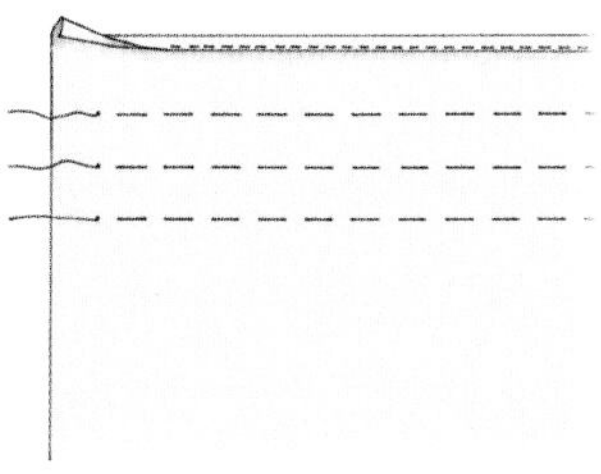

Diag 2

Pull up the pleating threads and tie off the panel to fit the following measurement

Size 1: 9 ¼" (23.5cm)

Size 2: 9 ⅞" (25cm)

Size 3: 10 ½" (26.5cm)

Size 4: 11" (28cm)

Smocking

See page 80 for the step-by-step instructions for cable stitch and page 90 for two step trellis stitch.

Count the pleats and mark the center valley.

Row 1 ½ - 2. Begin on the center two pleats on row 2 with an under cable. Two step trellis up to row 1 ½, over cable, two step trellis down to row 2. Continue to the end of the row. Turn the work upside down, return to the center and complete the row.

Row 1 ¼ - 1 ¾. Repeat the previous row a quarter space above.

Rows 2 - 2 ¾. Work a mirror image of the previous two rows.

Rows 9 ½ - 10 ½. Repeat rows 1 ½ - 2 and 2 - 2 ½.

Rows 10 ½ - 13. Following the graph for placement, work the partial rows of two step trellis, ending with a single diamond in the center between rows 12 and 13.

Row 11 - 14. Begin this row with an under cable on the center two pleats on row 14. Eight step trellis up to row 13, ten cables beginning with an over cable, eight step trellis up to row 12. Continue the cable/trellis combination until you reach row 11. Beginning with an over cable, work cable stitch to the end of the row. Turn the work upside down, return to the center and complete the row.

Preparation for Embroidery

Smocking

Remove the pleating threads. It is not recommended to block the smocking as it will crush the puffing between the upper and lower bands of smocking.

Shoulder straps

Using a ruler and the fabric marker, measure and mark two straps in the center of the piece of fabric, following the measurements on the pattern sheet. Mark the embroidery design with the rose 2 ⁵⁄₁₆" (6.5cm) up and 1 ³⁄₁₆" (3cm) away from the marked cutting lines on one end of both straps. Ensure you have a left and a right strap *(diag 3)*.

Diag 3

Buttons

Construct the top and attach the three center back buttons with a rosebud. The buttons on the end of the straps are not attached with embroidery as these may require adjustment as the child grows.

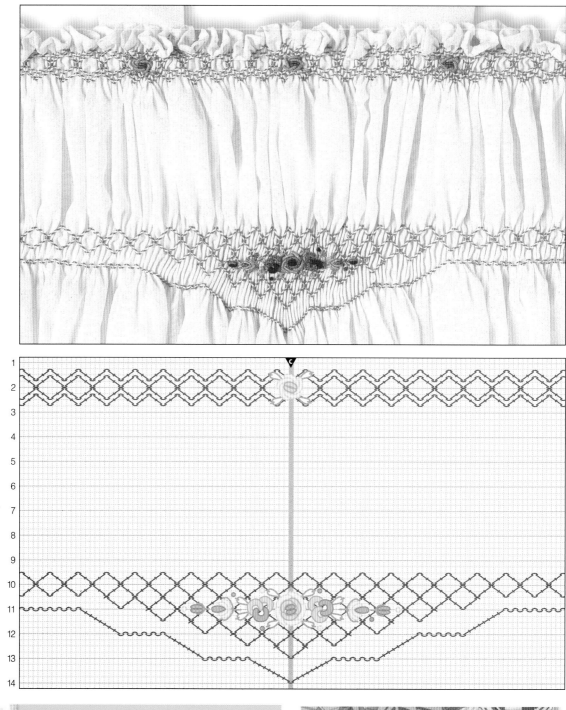

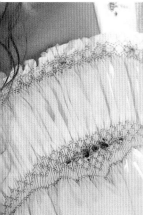

Color Key

DMC stranded cotton

A = 304 lt garnet
B = 471 vy lt avocado green
C = 841 lt beige
D = 3354 lt dusty rose
E = 3731 vy dk dusty rose
Smocking = C (3 strands)
Embroidery = A, B, D and E (2 strands)

Embroidery

See this page for the embroidery key.

See page 39 for step-by-step instructions for the cast-on stitch flowers, page 38 for instructions to attach a button with an embroidered rosebud and pages 88 and 89 for working bullion roses.

Embroidery on smocking

For all sizes, stitch a rose and four leaves in the junction between the center two diamonds on row 2. For sizes 3 and 4, work the same rose and leaves in the seventh junction either side of the center rose. This is the arrangement pictured on page 34. For sizes 1 and 2, work the roses and leaves in the sixth junction beside the center rose.

The side roses will be aligned with the placement of the shoulder straps during construction.

For the lower section of the design, begin with the center rose and work outwards. Use the graph as a guide for placing the individual elements of the embroidery.

Embroider the foliage after the rose, cast-on flowers and rosebuds are worked. Stitch two detached chains at each side of the rose. Link the cast-on stitch flowers to the rose with a single straight stitch, then work a pair of leaves on the remaining side of the flowers.

Stitch a detached chain on each side of the large rosebud for the sepals, then work a single straight stitch to connect the buds to the adjacent cast-on flower.

Work a fly stitch for the sepals of the small rosebuds, using a long anchoring stitch to link the buds to the top of the large rosebud. Scatter French knot buds around the design.

Shoulder straps

The large rose in the center of the main design on the smocking is repeated in the embroidery on the straps. Rosebuds extend above and below the rose, linked by the long anchoring stitch of the fly stitch sepals.

Detached chain leaves and French knot buds complete the design.

Buttons

A dainty rosebud with detached chain leaves, worked through the holes in the button, is used to attach the buttons at the center back of the top. Ensure the embroidery stitches are not pulled too tight as the button still requires a small amount of clearance under it to be functional without distorting the fabric.

Construction

See pages 100 - 102.

Embroidery Key

All embroidery is worked with two strands of thread.

Embroidery on smocking

Large rose

Center = A (2 bullion knots, 8 wraps)
Inner petals = E (3 bullion knots, 12 wraps)
Outer petals = D (5 - 6 bullion knots, 16 wraps)
Leaves = B (detached chain)

Cast-on stitch flowers

Petals = A or E (12 cast-ons)
Leaves = B (detached chain)

Small rose

Center = E (2 bullion knots, 8 wraps)
Outer petals = D (5 bullion knots 14 wraps)
Leaves = B (detached chain)

Large rosebud

Center = E (bullion knot, 8 wraps)
Outer petals = D (4 bullion knots 12 wraps)
Sepals and stem = B (detached chain straight stitch)

Small rosebud

Petals = A and E (2 bullion knots, 8 wraps)
Sepals and stem = B (fly stitch)

Scattered buds

Center = A, D and E (French knot, 3 wraps)

Shoulder straps

Large rose

Center = A (2 bullion knots, 8 wraps)
Inner petals = E (3 bullion knots, 12 wraps)
Outer petals = D (5 bullion knots, 16 wraps)
Leaves = B (detached chain)

Small rosebud

Petals = A and E (2 bullion knots, 8 wraps)
Sepals = B (fly stitch)

Buds

Center = D and E (French knot, 3 wraps)

Buttons

Rosebud

Center = E (bullion knot, 16 wraps)
Outer petals = D (2 bullion knots, 16 wraps)
Leaves = B (detached chain)

This charming little bracelet is the essential accessory for the top and pants. As the bracelet contains beads and small findings, it may pose a choking risk to the child if the joins are not made securely.

Requirements

Beads

4 x ³⁄₁₆" (4mm) white glass beads
4 x ¼" (6mm) green glass beads
7 x ³⁄₁₆" (4mm) pink glass faceted beads
7 x ³⁄₁₆" (4mm) champagne glass faceted beads
2 silver crimp beads
19 silver lined glass seed beads

Findings

1 silver head pin
8 antique silver bead caps
1 silver parrot clasp
1 x ¼" (6mm) silver split jump ring

Notions

8" (20cm) silver flexible beading wire
Chain nose or flat nose pliers
Round nose pliers
Wire cutters

Making the bracelet

String a crimp bead and the clasp onto one end of the wire, then take the wire back through the crimp bead leaving a ³⁄₈" (1cm) tail *(diag 1)*.

Diag 1

With the crimp bead as close as possible to the clasp, use the chain nosed pliers to flatten the bead. Check that the bead is secure and doesn't slide along the wire *(diag 2)*. If necessary, reposition and flatten again.

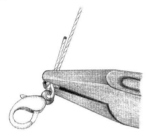

Diag 2

Thread one white glass bead, glass seed bead, champagne faceted bead, glass seed bead, pink faceted bead and one glass seed bead onto the wire. Push them to meet the crimp bead, covering the tail of wire below the bead *(diag 3)*.

Diag 3

Thread on a bead cap (closed end first), a green glass bead, bead cap (open end first), glass seed bead, pink faceted bead, glass seed bead, champagne faceted bead, glass seed bead, white glass bead, glass seed bead, champagne faceted bead, glass seed bead, pink faceted bead and then another glass seed bead *(diag 4)*.

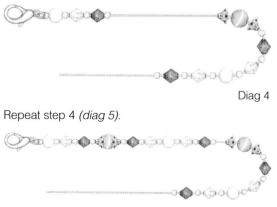

Diag 4

Repeat step 4 *(diag 5)*.

Diag 5

The bracelet is approximately 5 ½" (14cm) long from the jump ring to the clasp.
Add or subtract beads to adjust the length if necessary.

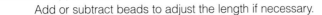

Thread on a bead cap (closed end first), a green glass bead, bead cap (open end first), glass seed bead, pink faceted bead, glass seed bead, champagne faceted bead, glass seed bead, white glass bead and the second crimp bead (diag 6).

Diag 6

Grasp the wire at the bend with the round-nosed pliers. Bring the wire up and around the tip of the pliers with your fingers (diag 10).

Diag 10

Leaving a ⅝" (1.5cm) tail of wire, cut off the excess with the wire cutters. Pass the end of the wire through the jump ring and then back through the crimp bead and the other beads until the tail is completely hidden (diag 7). Use the chain-nosed pliers to flatten the crimp bead as in step 2.

Re-position the pliers so that the lower jaw is in the loop. Then bring the tail of wire under the pliers to form a right angle with the stem (diag 11).

Diag 11

Diag 7

Beaded Drop

Thread a seed bead, pink faceted bead, bead cap (closed end first), green glass bead, bead cap (open end first) and a champagne faceted bead onto the head pin (diag 8).

Diag 8

Re-position the pliers across the loop and hold it firmly. Wrap the tail around the stem (diag 12).

Diag 12

Using the chain-nosed pliers bend the pin at a right angle just above the top of the last bead (diag 9).

Trim the tail of wire. Press the cut end close under the wraps with the chain-nosed pliers. Place the beaded drop onto the split ring by threading it through the coils of the ring (diag 13).

Diag 9

Diag 13

This decorative method of attaching buttons adds the perfect finishing touch to the top.

1. Position the button on the fabric so the holes form a diamond. Secure the thread on the back. Bring it to the front through upper hole (A).

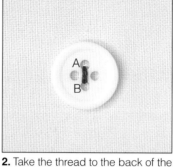

2. Take the thread to the back of the fabric through the lower hole (B). Pull the thread firmly to anchor the button.

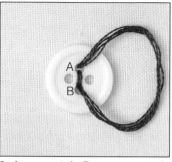

3. Inner petal. Re-emerge at A. Take the needle to the back at B. Pull the thread through, leaving a large loop on the front.

4. Re-emerge at A and leave the needle in the button. Hold the needle firmly on the back of the fabric with your left hand.

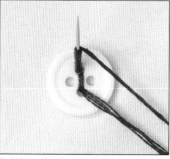

5. Wrap the loop of thread around the needle in a clockwise direction for the required number of wraps. Ensure they are evenly packed together.

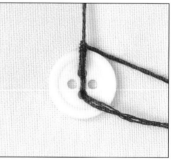

6. Holding the wraps securely, carefully pull the thread through.

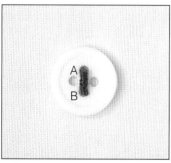

7. Pull the thread towards you until wraps are even and lie firmly against the button. Take the thread to the back at B and secure.

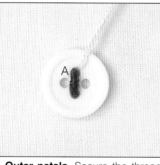

8. Outer petals. Secure the thread on the back and emerge at A, just to the right of the inner petal.

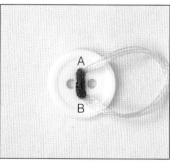

9. Take the needle to the back at B, just to the right of the inner petal. Pull the thread through leaving a large loop on the front as before.

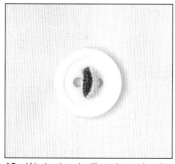

10. Work the bullion knot in the same manner as the inner petal. Ensure it lies to the right of the inner petal.

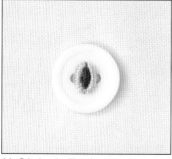

11. Stitch a bullion knot on the left of the inner petal in the same manner to complete the bud.

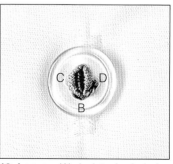

12. Leaves. Work detached chains from B to C and B to D. Secure the thread on the back.

Cast-on Stitch Flowers

Cast-on stitch is used in Brazilian embroidery which makes extensive use of raised stitches. Each cast-on stitch consists of a number of loops cast onto the needle and then anchored to the fabric. The work is rotated as each stitch is formed.

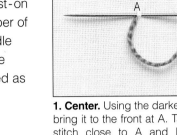

1. Center. Using the darkest shade, bring it to the front at A. Take a tiny stitch close to A and leave the needle in the fabric.

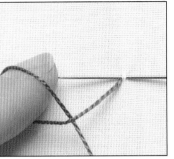

2. Keeping the tension on the thread, place your finger tip on the point of the needle.

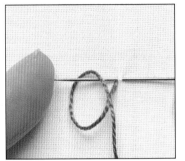

3. Slip the loop off your finger and onto the needle.

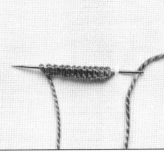

4. Continue until the required number of cast-ons are on the needle.

5. Hold the cast-ons in your left hand. With your right hand, pull the needle and thread through the stitches.

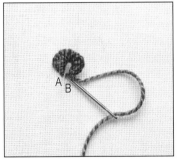

6. To anchor the stitch, take the needle to the back at B, close to where the needle last emerged.

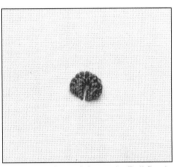

7. Pull the thread through. Pull firmly but do not let the fabric pucker. End off the thread.

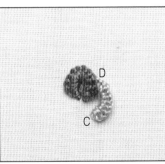

8. Work a second petal from C to D (D is directly behind A and B).

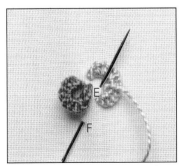

9. Keeping the first petal out of the way, bring the thread to the front at E. Work another petal from F to E.

Gorgeous floral pajamas -
perfect for a slumber party!

Shabby Chic

By **Julie Graue**

The pajama top features a dainty smocked frill, embroidered with petite floral accents, bordering the pocket on the left front. The dusky aqua blue striped fabric used for the pocket, upper collar and facings on the top and three-quarter length pants, provides the perfect contrast for the floral print. The curved splits of the top and pants are decorated with tiny aqua bows. The elastic casing of the pants is complemented by a pretty satin ribbon drawstring.

Requirements

Sizes 8, 10 & 12 years

Fabric

Cremé floral cotton print 44" (112cm) wide

Size 8 : 83" (2.1m)

Size 10 : 86 ⅝" (2.2m)

Size 12 : 90 ½" (2.3m)

Antique aqua stripe cotton, 27 ½" x 44" wide (70cm x 112cm) for all sizes

Notions

17 ¾" x 23 ⅝" wide (45cm x 60cm) piece of lightweight woven fusible interfacing

47 ¼" x ⅜" wide (1.2m x 10mm) pale aqua satin ribbon

22" x ³⁄₁₆" wide (56cm x 4mm) pale aqua satin ribbon

21 ⅝" x ¾" wide (55cm x 20mm) white non-roll elastic

4 x ¾" (18mm) aqua buttons

Fine tip water-soluble fabric marker

No. 7 crewel needle (smocking)

No. 9 milliner's needle (embroidery)

Threads

See page 44.

Pattern

See the liftout pattern sheets.

We recommend that you read the complete article and the pattern instructions relating to this project before you begin.

The finished back length of the top is

Size 8: 19 ¼" (49cm)

Size 10: 20" (51cm)

Size 12: 20 ¾" (53cm)

The finished side length of the three-quarter pants is

Size 8: 22 ¼" (56.5cm)

Size 10: 23 ¼" (59cm)

Size 12: 24 ¼" (61.5cm)

There is no hem allowance on either garment.

Cutting out

See the pattern sheet for the cutting layouts.

Antique aqua stripe cotton

Pocket frill: cut one, 2 ½" x 12 ⅝" wide (6.5cm x 32cm) for all sizes

Trace the pattern pieces onto lightweight interfacing or tracing paper, transferring the pattern markings. Cut out the remaining pieces following the instructions on the pattern sheet.

Preparation and Pleating

Using the fabric marker, rule a line down the center of the length of striped fabric cut for the pocket frill. Using threads longer than the width of the fabric and aligning the center needle with the marked line, pleat 5 half space rows. This includes an upper and a lower holding row.

Unpick the pleating threads for 1" (2.5cm) at one side. Count 42 pleats and unpick the remaining pleats. Leaving 1" (2.5cm) of flat fabric past the last pleat, trim the excess, taking care not to cut the pleating threads.

Flatten out the pleats. Fold under a narrow double hem on both raw edges of the frill and machine stitch *(diag 1)*. Press.

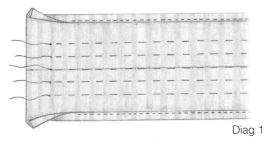

Diag 1

Pull up the pleats and tie off the panel to measure 4 ⅜" (11cm) wide.

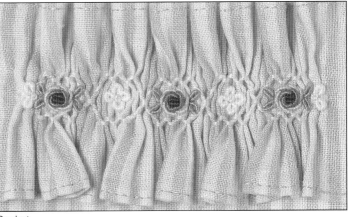

Pocket

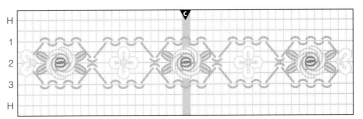

Sleeve

Smocking

See page 45 for the step-by-step instructions to stitch the five cable/wave combination and page 80 for cable stitch.

All rows are worked from left to right.

Row 1 - 2. Begin on the left hand side with an under cable on row 2, wave up to row 1, five cables (over, under, over, under, over), wave down to row 2. Continue to the end of the row.

Row 2 - 3. Work a mirror image of the previous row.

Backsmocking

Using two strands, work cable stitch along rows 1 and 3 on the back of the fabric.

Hint

Always wash your fabrics in hot water to pre-shrink them before use. 100% cotton fabrics are particularly susceptible to shrinkage.

Embroidery

See this page for the embroidery key.

See pages 88 and 89 for the step-by-step instructions for working bullion roses.

Rinse away all traces of the fabric marker and leave the panel to dry. Press the edges of the frill carefully.

Following the graph for placement, stitch a rose in the center and at each end of the smocking. Embroider a pair of bullion stitch leaves on each side of each rose. Stitch a four-petalled bullion loop daisy in the spaces between the roses and a partial daisy at each end.

Construction

See pages 102 - 104.

Pants leg

Hint

Rinse away fabric marker with cold water and avoid ironing any marked areas as heat may set the marker into the fabric.

Color Key

Presencia stranded cotton

A = 1137 lt yellow

B = 1645 vy lt cranberry

C = 1651 cranberry

D = 1661 dk cranberry

E = 3000 ecru

F = 3639 lt aqua

G = 5140 sage

Smocking = F (3 strands)

Backsmocking = F (2 strands)

Embroidery = A, B, C, D, E and G

Embroidery Key

All embroidery is worked with two strands of thread unless otherwise specified.

Roses

Center = D (2 bullion knots, 10 wraps)

Inner petals = C (3 bullion knots 10 wraps)

Outer petals = B (6 bullion knots, 10 wraps)

Leaves = G (2 bullion knots, 10 wraps)

Daisies

Petals = E (2 or 4 bullion loops, 25 wraps)

Center = A (3 strands, French knot)

Combining smocking stitches opens up limitless design opportunities.

This five cable/wave combination is worked between two half space pleating rows. The row is then mirror-imaged and the resulting hexagons form the perfect frame for the embroidered flowers.

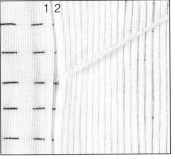

1. Bring the thread to the front on row 2 between the first two pleats.

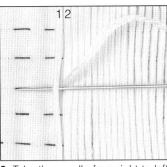

2. Take the needle from right to left through the first pleat.

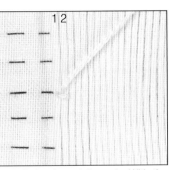

3. Pull the thread through. With the thread below the needle, take the needle through pleat two and work an under cable.

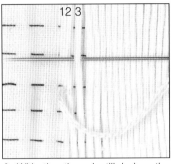

4. With the thread still below the needle, take the needle through pleat three on row 1.

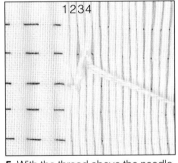

5. With the thread above the needle, work an over cable on pleats three and four.

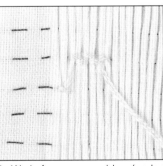

6. Work four more cables (under, over, under, over).

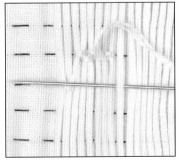

7. With the thread above the needle, wave down to row 2.

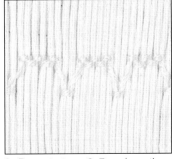

8. Repeat steps 3-7 and continue working this sequence to the end of the row.

Crisp white cotton dress and vest
with sequins, beads and ruffles

Summer Breeze

By **Julie Graue**

Tiers of lighter-than-air embroidered voile create a breathtaking summer dress and matching vest. Sparkling beads and sequins accentuate the embroidered paisley motifs on the vest fabric.

Requirements

Sizes 4, 6, 8 and 10 years

Fabric

White embroidered cotton voile (swirls) 44" (112cm) wide
Sizes 4 and 6: 67" (1.7m)
Sizes 8 and 10: 75 ¾" (2m)
White embroidered cotton voile (paisley) 44" (112cm) wide
Sizes 4 and 6: 55" (1.4m)
Sizes 8 and 10: 67" (1.7m)
51 ¼" x 44" wide (1.3m x 112cm) white cotton voile for all sizes

Notions

4" x 8" wide (10cm x 20cm) piece of lightweight woven fusible interfacing
138" x ⅜" wide (3.5m x 10mm) white satin ribbon
29 ½" x ¼" wide (75cm x 6mm) white satin ribbon
2 x ½" (13mm) white buttons
2 x ⁵⁄₁₆" (8mm) white glass beads
Beading thread for embroidery
Fine tip water-soluble fabric marker
No. 8 crewel needle (backsmocking)
No. 9 milliner's needle (beaded smocking)

Threads, beads and sequins

See page 50.

Pattern

See the liftout pattern sheet.

We recommend that you read the complete article and the pattern instructions relating to this project before you begin.

The finished back length of the dress from the shoulder to the hemline is
Size 4: 30" (76cm)
Size 6: 32" (81cm)
Size 8: 34" (86cm)
Size 10: 36" (91cm)

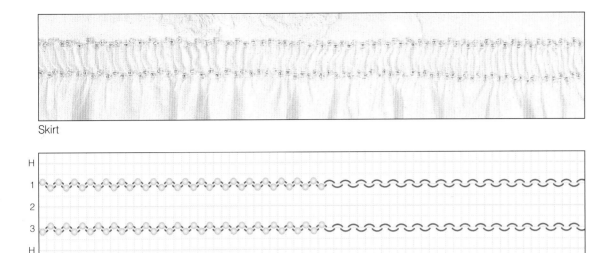

Skirt

The finished back length of the vest is

Size 4: 10 ⅝" (27cm)

Size 6: 11 ⅝" (29.5cm)

Size 8: 12 ⅝" (32cm)

Size 10: 13 ⅝" (34.5cm)

There is no hem allowance on either garment.

Cutting out

See the pattern sheet for the cutting layouts.

White embroidered cotton voile (swirls)

Skirt upper tier: cut two, each

Size 4: 8 ⅝" x 38 ⅝" wide (22cm x 98cm)

Size 6: 9 ⅝" x 38 ⅝" wide (24.5cm x 98cm)

Size 8: 10 ⅝" x 44" wide (27cm x 112cm)

Size 10: 11 ⅝" x 44" wide (29.5cm x 112cm)

Trace the pattern pieces onto lightweight interfacing or tracing paper, transferring the pattern markings. Cut out the remaining pieces following the instructions on the pattern sheet.

Preparation and pleating

Fold one of the skirt upper tier pieces in half across the width. Finger press the fold. Open out and mark the foldline, 4 ⅜" (11cm) down from the upper edge. This will be the back skirt piece.

With right sides together and matching raw edges, stitch the two skirt upper tier pieces together at one side. Trim and neaten the seam. Press to one side.

Pleat 5 half space rows (including two holding rows) with the top holding row ⅜" (1cm) from the upper raw edge.

Unpick the pleating threads for ⅜" (1cm) at each side for the seam allowance. Pull up the pleating threads and tie off to fit the combined width of the front and back bodice pattern pieces (minus the seam allowances).

On the back skirt piece, flatten the pleats either side of the marked line. Leaving at least ¼" (6mm) seam

allowance on both sides of the line, mark the first pleat on each side with the fabric marker *(diag 1)*.

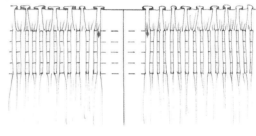

Diag 1

The smocking begins and ends on these pleats, leaving the space between to insert the placket.

Smocking

See page 51 for the step-by-step instructions for beaded cable stitch.

There are two panels to smock. One, the front skirt plus half the back and then the remaining half of the back. The smocking can be worked from one side of the panels to the other, remembering to stop and begin again on the marked pleats at the center back.

Row 1. Work beaded cable stitch across the row.

Row 3. Stitch a mirror image of the previous row.

Backsmocking

Using two strands, work cable stitch along rows 1 and 3 on the back of the fabric.

Hint

Before pleating fine fabrics, lightly spray starch and press to give the fabric more body.

Preparation for embroidery

Stitch the shoulder seams of the vest following the instructions on page 106.

Embroidery

Crystal seed beads and sequins add a delicate sparkle to the machine embroidery on the fabric used for the vest.

Look at the individual motifs embroidered on the fabric and decide where to place the beads and sequins to enhance the design.

Attach the sequins with a seed bead. Knot the beading thread securely. Position the sequin and bring the thread to the front through the hole in the center. Thread a seed bead and take the needle to the back through the sequin again (*diag 2*). Pull tight.

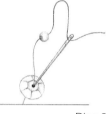

Diag 2

End off between beads or secure the thread on the back and carry it to the next position.

Construction

See pages 105 - 107.

Color Key
DMC stranded cotton
A = B5200 bright white
Mill Hill glass seed beads
B = 02010 ice
Maria George crystal faceted sequins
C = 6mm (¼") white
Smocking = A (2 strands) and B
Backsmocking = A (2 strands)
Embroidery = B and C

Hint

Secure the thread on the back before attaching the next bead in a sequence. This will ensure that you won't lose too many beads if the thread should break with wear and tear.

Embellishing your smocking designs with beads, adds an element of glamour or sparkle. They can be added in many ways but here, tiny seed beads have been incorporated into the stitches.

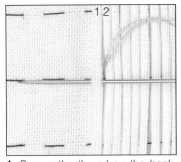

1. Secure the thread on the back. Bring it to the front between pleats 1 and 2. Take the needle from right to left through the first pleat.

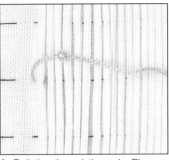

2. Pull the thread through. Place a bead on the thread.

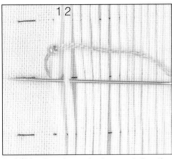

3. With the thread above, take the needle from right to left through pleat 2.

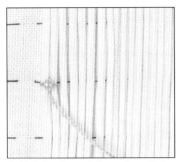

4. Pull the thread through until the bead rests on the fabric.

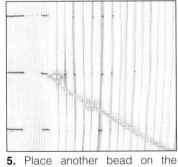

5. Place another bead on the thread.

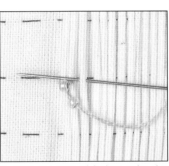

6. With the thread below, take the needle from right to left through the next pleat.

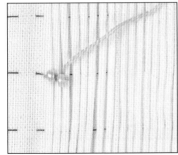

7. Pull the thread through until the bead rests on the fabric.

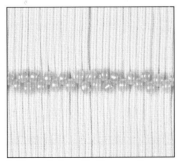

8. Repeat steps 2 - 7 across the row.

Freewheeling fun... a sophisticated summer look for girls with flair

First Love

By **Jennie Victorsen**

This casual, front-buttoning top, worn over jeans or leggings, is smocked at the front waistline and shirred at the back. Chunky beads and fabric flowers create a trendy necklace to complete the outfit.

Requirements

Sizes 10, 12 and 14 years

Fabric

43 ¼" x 59" wide (1.1m x 150cm)
red with white spot polyester jersey for all sizes

Notions

White shirring elastic
2 x ⅜" (10mm) clear plastic buttons
75/4mm twin machine needle for stretch fabrics
No. 8 crewel needle (smocking)

Threads

See opposite page.

Pattern

See the liftout pattern sheet.

We recommend that you read the complete article and the pattern instructions relating to this project before you begin.

The finished length from the center back neckline to the hemline is

Size 10: 24 ¾" (63cm)
Size 12: 26 ⅜" (67cm)
Size 14: 28" (71cm)

There is no hem allowance.

Cutting out

See the pattern sheet for the cutting layout.

Red with white spot polyester jersey

Front skirt: cut one, 32 ¾" (83cm) wide
Size 10: 15 ¾" (40cm)
Size 12: 17" (43cm)
Size 14: 18 ⅛" (46cm)

Trace the pattern pieces onto lightweight interfacing or tracing paper, transferring the pattern markings. Cut out the remaining pieces following the instructions on the pattern sheet.

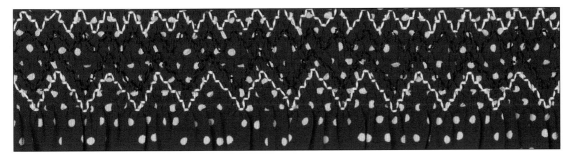

Skirt

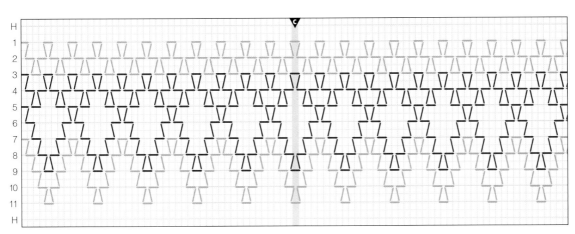

Pleating

Pleat 13 half space rows (including two holding rows) with the top row ⅜" (1cm) from the upper raw edge.

Unpick the pleating threads for ⅝" (1.5cm) at each side. Tie off to fit the following measurement

Size 10: 11" (28cm)

Size 12: 11 ¾" (30cm)

Size 14: 12 ½" (32cm)

Smocking

See pages 86 and 87 for the step-by-step instructions for double and stepped Van Dyke stitch.

Count the pleats and mark the center valley.

Row 1 - 3. Bring the thread to the front on the right hand side of the pleat to the right of the center valley, then use the center two pleats on row 1 to begin the Van Dyke stitch. Step down to row 2, with the thread above, stitch twice from right to left through the first and second pleats left of center, step down to row 3 and repeat the stitches through the second and third pleats. Step up to row 2, with the thread below, stitch twice through the third and fourth pleats. Step up to row 1 and work two stitches as before through the fourth and fifth pleats. Continue to the end of the row. Turn the work, return to the center and complete the row.

Row 3 - 5. Change thread color. Beginning on the right hand side of the panel and following the graph for stitch placement, repeat the previous row.

Row 5 - 9. Begin stitching on the center two pleats on row 9, step up to row 5 by placing stitches through two pleats, one old and one new, on rows 8, 7, 6 and 5. Continue working Van Dyke stitch, stepping up and down between rows 5 and 9. Turn the work, return to the center and complete the row.

Row 7 - 11. Change thread color. Beginning on the right hand side of the panel and following the graph for stitch placement, repeat the previous row.

Backsmocking

Using cable stitch, backsmock along the upper holding row and rows 6, 7, 10 and 11.

Construction

See pages 107 - 109.

Color Key

Anchor stranded cotton

A = 1 snow white

B = 150 blue navy

C = 1006 bright garnet

Smocking = A and B (3 strands)

Backsmocking = C (3 strands)

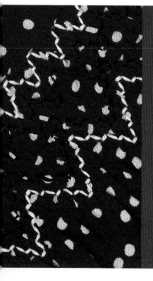

The finished necklace measures 37 ⅜" (95cm).

The Necklace

This simple necklace is fashioned from scraps of fabric and a coordinating assortment of beads.

Requirements

Fabric

4" x 10 ⅝" wide (10cm x 27cm) piece of blue denim

3 ⅛" x 9" wide (8cm x 23cm) piece of red with white spot polyester jersey

Beads

15 x ¼" (6mm) red wooden beads

3 x ¾" (20mm) wooden beads covered with white needlelace

6 x ¾" (2cm) flat clear glass beads with red accents

Notions

39 ⅜" (1m) thick white cotton piping cord

Large beading or milliner's needle

Thread

47 ¼" (1.2m) red perlé thread or 3 strands of red stranded cotton.

Beginning and ending a new thread in Van Dyke stitch

The best place to end off and begin again is at the point where two stitches are placed over two pleats.

To end off, take the first stitch through two pleats as usual. Then take the needle and thread to the back on the right hand pleat, through the same hole as the first stitch (*diag 1*).

Secure the thread on the back.

To begin a new thread, secure it on the back and bring the needle and thread to the front on the left hand side of the right pleat, through the same hole as the first stitch (*diag 2*).

Continue stitching.

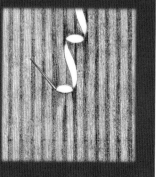

Construction

Using the templates on the pattern sheet, cut three small flowers from the spot fabric and three large flowers from the denim. Knot the ends of the white cord.

Cut three 15 ¾" (40cm) lengths of the red thread.

1. Central floral motif. String three red wooden beads, a flat glass bead, two red beads, a needlelace bead, then two red beads onto a length of red thread.

2. Omitting the last red bead, pass the thread back through the beads. Center the string of beads on the doubled thread.

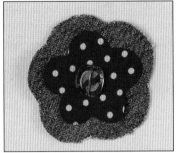

3. Center one spotted flower over one denim flower. Attach a flat glass bead in the center of the flowers, securing them together.

4. Thread the string of beads onto a needle and take it through the glass bead on the flower.

5. Pull the thread until the string of beads is close to the glass bead on the flower. End off the thread securely on the back.

6. Side floral motifs. Make two more flowers following the instructions in step 3.

7. Make two strands of beads with one red bead, one flat glass bead, one red bead, one white needlelace bead and two red beads as before.

8. Attaching the flowers and bead strands. Using white thread, stitch the center motif in the center of the cord.

9. Thread a small bead strand onto a needle and secure it to the cord 2 ½" (6.5cm) left of the center motif. Secure the remaining strand the same distance right of center.

10. Attach the side floral motifs 2" (5cm) away from the bead strands.

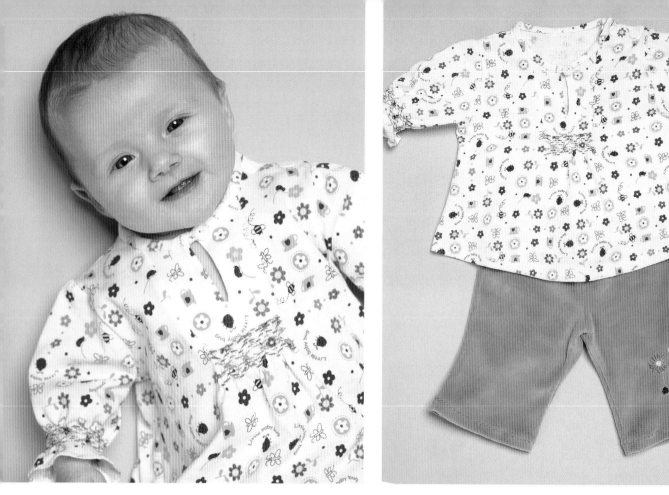

Ladybird, ladybird, fly away home...

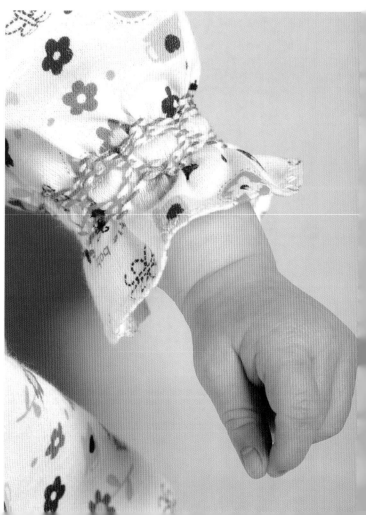

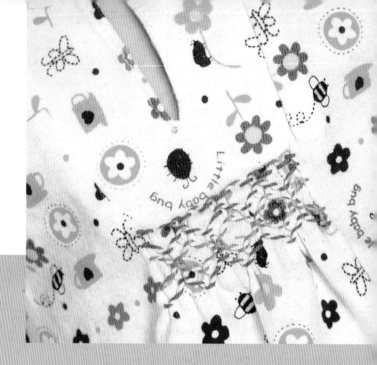

Little Baby Bug

By **Cathy Gunn**

There is just a hint of whimsy in the printed design of this cotton knit smocked top. The delightful insects and floral theme of the print are mirrored in the embroidery on the soft velour pants.

Requirements

Sizes newborn, 3, 6 and 12 months

Fabric

Cotton knit print 59" (150cm) wide

Sizes newborn and 3 months: 17 ¾" (45cm)

Sizes 6 and 12 months: 19 ¾" (50cm)

Strawberry pink velour

Sizes newborn and 3 months:
15 ¾" x 31 ½" wide (40cm x 80cm)

Sizes 6 and 12 months:
17 ¾" x 35 ½" wide (45cm x 90cm)

Notions

17 ¾" x ¾" wide (45cm x 20mm) white non-roll elastic

1 x ⅜" (10mm) white button

2 ivory popper studs

Fine tip water-soluble fabric marker

No. 7 crewel needle (smocking)

No. 8 milliner's needle (embroidery)

Threads

See opposite page.

Pattern

See the liftout pattern sheet.

We recommend that you read the complete article and the pattern instructions relating to this project before you begin.

The finished back length of the top is

Size newborn: 10" (25.5cm)

Size 3 months: 11 ¼" (28.5cm)

Size 6 months: 12 ⅜" (31.5cm)

Size 12 months: 13 ⅝" (34.5cm)

The finished side length of the pants is

Size newborn: 11" (28cm)

Size 3 months: 12 ⅝" (32cm)

Size 6 months: 14 ¼" (36cm)

Size 12 months: 15 ¾" (40cm)

There is no hem allowance on either garment.

Cutting out

See the pattern sheet for the cutting layouts.

Cotton knit print

Top front rectangle: cut one,

Size newborn: 13 ¾" x 17 ¾" wide (35cm x 45cm)

Size 3 months: 15" x 19" wide (38cm x 48cm)

Size 6 months: 16 ⅛" x 20" wide (41cm x 51cm)

Size 12 months: 17 ⅜" x 21 ¼" wide (44cm x 54cm)

The front will be cut to shape after the smocking is complete.

Trace the pattern pieces onto lightweight interfacing or tracing paper, transferring the pattern markings. Cut out the remaining pieces following the instructions on the pattern sheet.

Preparation & pleating

Front

Fold the rectangle cut for the top front in half down the length and finger press the fold. Open out the rectangle. Using the fabric marker, rule a line down the center front following the foldline.

Transfer the top front shaping onto both halves of the rectangle and rule a line at the position marked

Diag 1

on the top front pattern piece *(diag 1).*

Pleat 7 half space rows (including two holding rows) aligning the top holding row along the horizontal marked line *(diag 2).*

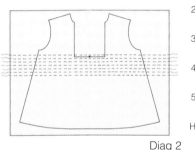

Diag 2

This design uses 18 pleats. Count 9 pleats either side of the center front and unpick the remaining pleats. Tie off the pleated area to measure 2" (5cm) wide.

Sleeves

Using threads longer than the width of the sleeve, pleat 7 half space rows on the lower edge of each sleeve, with the lower holding row ¾" (2cm) from the raw edge. Flatten out the pleats. Fold under 3/16" (4mm) on the raw edge and zigzag the hem in place.

Unpick the pleating threads for ⅜" (1cm) at each side for the seam allowance. Pull up the pleating threads and tie off the pleated area to measure 4" (10cm) wide.

Smocking

See page 80 for the step-by-step instructions for cable stitch and page 85 for half space wave stitch forming diamonds.

Front

Row 1 - 2. Beginning on the left hand side, and following the graph for stitch placement and thread color, work half space wave across the row.

Row 2 - 3. Changing thread color, repeat the previous row.

Rows 3 - 5. Stitch a mirror image of rows 1 - 3.

Row 1. Following the graph, work a row of cable stitch immediately above the first row of wave stitch.

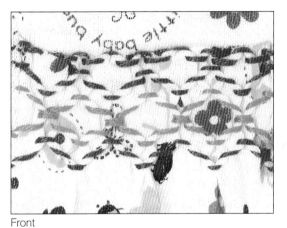

Front

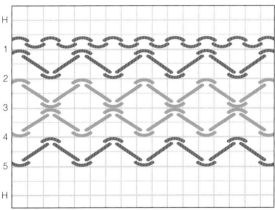

Color Key

DMC stranded cotton

A = 310 black

B = 321 vy lt garnet

C = 727 lt golden yellow

D = 741 med tangerine

E = 907 lt parrot green

F = 3607 fuchsia

Smocking = D and F (3 strands)

Embroidery = A, B, C, D and E

Sleeves

Count the pleats and mark the center valley.

Row 1 - 2. Begin with an over cable on the center two pleats on row 1. Wave down to row 2, under cable, wave up to row 1. Continue to the end of the row. Turn the work upside down, return to the center and complete the row.

Row 2 - 3. Changing thread color, repeat the previous row.

Rows 3 - 5. Stitch a mirror image of rows 1 - 3.

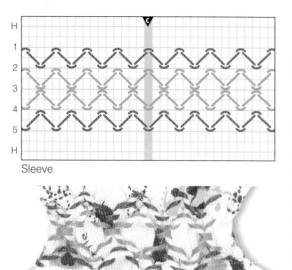

Sleeve

Preparation for embroidery

See the liftout pattern sheet for the embroidery design.
Fold the left front pants in half at the lower leg. Tack a line 4 ¾" (12cm) up from the lower edge on the fold. Trace the design onto the tracing paper. Pierce holes in the tracing at ¼" (6mm) intervals along the stem and the outer circle of the flower with a large needle. Pierce holes at the top and base of the leaves and the bee's body and wings.

Matching the tacked line and markings, pin the tracing to the pants with the base of the stem 1 ¾" (4.5cm) up from the lower raw edge. Using the fabric marker, dot through the holes in the tracing to transfer the markings. Remove the tracing and join the dots to provide a framework to stitch the embroidery. Draw a ¼" (6mm) circle in the middle of the large circle for the flower center. Remove the tacking.

Ladybird

The ladybird is stitched entirely in bullion knots, six for the body and two for the head.

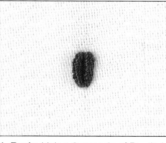

1. Body. Using 2 strands of B, stitch a vertical 12 wrap bullion knot. Work a second knot beside the first.

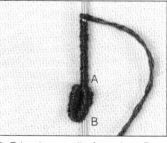

2. Take the needle from A to B on one side of the central knots. Place 16 wraps on the needle.

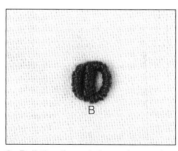

3. Pull the thread through, curving the stitch outwards. Take the thread to the back at B.

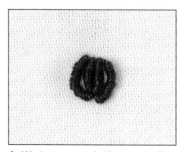

4. Work a second 16 wrap bullion knot on the remaining side of the central bullion knots in the same manner.

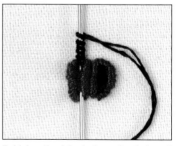

5. Using the black thread, stitch a 6 wrap bullion inside each curved outer bullion knot for the spots.

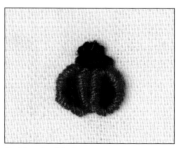

6. Head. Stitch a 10 wrap bullion across the top of the body. Finish the head with a 6 wrap bullion, centering the stitch above the previous knot.

Embroidery

See the opposite page for step-by-step instructions for stitching the ladybird and this page for the bee.

Work the stem in outline stitch and the leaves in detached chain. For each leaf, work two detached chains, one inside the other. Work the right hand leaf with stitches a little looser than the left to make room for the ladybird.

Embroider 17 bullion knots for the flower petals, varying the length of the stitches and allowing some to overlap the others. Stitch bullion knots at the 12, 3, 6 and 9 o'clock positions between the inner and outer circles, then work another 3 or 4 bullions between. Fill the center with French knots.

Stitch the ladybird on the right hand leaf following the step-by-step instructions.

Embroider the bee following the step-by-step instructions below.

Construction

See pages 109 - 111.

Bee

Bullion knots, detached chain and straight stitch are used to create the bee.

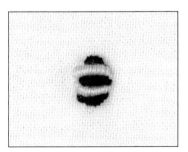

1. Body. Using 3 strands of C and leaving space for a knot between, stitch two 12 wrap bullion knots for the center of the bee's body.

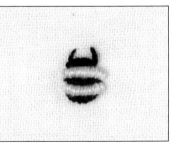

2. Using two strands of A, work an 8 wrap bullion at one end of the body, centering it on the first yellow knot.

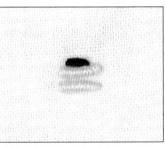

3. Next, work a 12 wrap bullion between the two yellow knots.

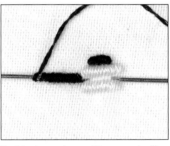

4. Work a second 8 wrap bullion at the other end of the body.

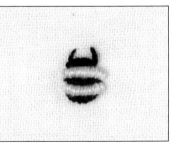

5. Feelers. Work two tiny straight stitches, angled towards each other, at the top of the body.

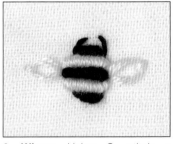

6. Wings. Using C, stitch a detached chain on each side of the body, anchoring the stitches away from the bee, taking care not to pull them too tight.

Shop in style with this floral skirt and embroidered bag

Born to Shop

By **Debbie Shepherd**

Accessorize this stylish flounced skirt with a matching shoulder bag. This would make the perfect project for a mother-daughter team. The bag is simple enough for a beginner, while someone more experienced could make the skirt.

Requirements for skirt

Sizes 8, 10, 12 and 14 years

Fabric

55" x 59" wide (1.4m x 150cm) floral cotton print for all sizes

Notions

10" x 40" wide (25cm x 100cm) piece of lightweight woven fusible interfacing

8" (20cm) ivory zipper

Hook and eye

No. 7 crewel needle (smocking)

Threads

See page 68.

Pattern

See the liftout pattern sheet.

We recommend that you read the complete article and the instructions relating to this project before you begin.

The finished back length of the skirt is

Size 8: 14 ½" (37cm)

Size 10: 15 ⅛" (38.5cm)

Size 12: 15 ¾" (40cm)

Size 14: 16 ⅜" (41.5cm)

There is no hem allowance.

Cutting out

See the liftout pattern sheet for the cutting layout.

Floral cotton print

Front yoke: cut one, 6 ⅛" x 59" wide (15.5cm x 150cm) for all sizes

Trace the pattern pieces onto lightweight interfacing or tracing paper, transferring the pattern markings. Cut out the remaining pieces following the instructions on the pattern sheet.

Pleating

Pleat 14 full space rows (including two upper and two lower holding rows) with the top holding row ⅜" (1cm) from the upper raw edge.

Unpick the pleating threads for ⅜" (1cm) at each side. Tie off the panel to fit the front yoke blocking guide.

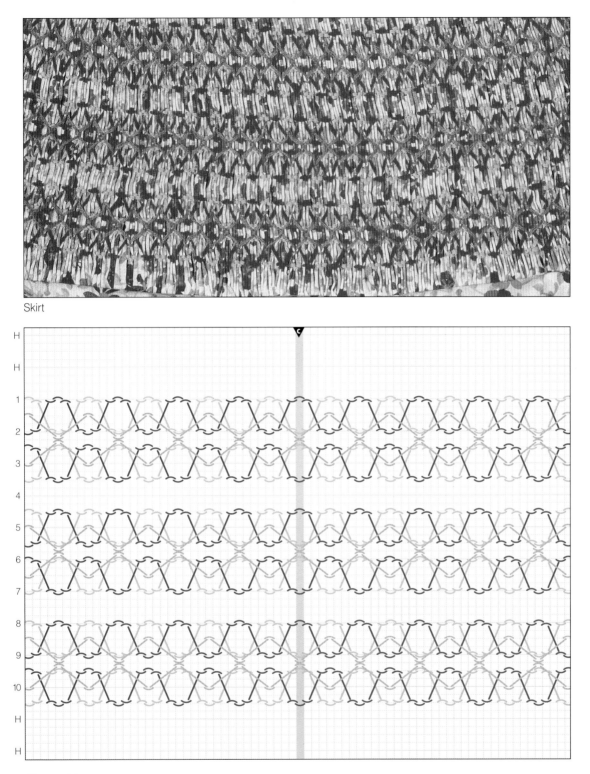

Skirt

Smocking

See pages 68 and 69 for the step-by-step instructions for the three cable/wave variation.

Layered rows of crossover stitches, using vibrant colors to match the fabric, form the three bands of smocking that feature in this colorful design. The pale green rows are worked first, then the red and finally the bright orange rows to complete the design.

Count the pleats and mark the center valley.

Row 1 - 2. Using the green thread, begin on the center two pleats on row 2 with an under cable. Work another cable with the thread below the needle. Wave up to row 1 and stitch three cables following steps 3 - 9 on pages 68 and 69. Wave down to row 2 and stitch three cables following steps 9 - 11 on page 69. Continue to the end of the row. Turn the work upside down, return to the center and complete the row.

Using the dark pink thread and following the graph for placement, repeat the previous row, placing the stitches on the free pleats between the stitching of the previous row.

Rows 2 ½ - 3 ½. Work a mirror image of the previous two rows, using the same color sequence and leaving a half-space between the bands.

Rows 1 ½ - 3. Following the graph for placement and using the orange thread, work mirror image rows of wave stitch over the previous four rows.

Rows 4 ½ - 7 and 8 - 10 ½. Repeat rows 1 - 3 ½ twice, leaving a full space between each band of stitching.

Backsmocking

Using the green thread, backsmock in cable along the holding rows.

Construction

See pages 111 - 113.

Color Key
DMC stranded cotton
A = 326 vy deep rose
Anchor stranded cotton
B = 255 yellow-green
C = 316 orange
Smocking = A, B and C (3 strands)
Backsmocking = B (2 strands)

The background rows in this design are a variation on a classic three cable/wave combination. In this instance, the three cables (a cable picot) are stitched facing outwards from the wave rather than the cable picots facing inwards. The cable/wave combination, together with a simple wave stitch, has been stitched in crossover layers to build up the intensity of the stitching against the dense background of the floral fabric.

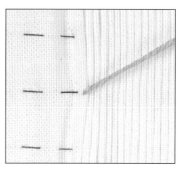

1. Bring the thread to the front in a valley. Take the needle from left to right through the pleat to the left. Pull the thread through to begin stitching.

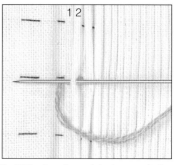

2. With the thread below and the needle horizonal, take it from right to left through the second pleat.

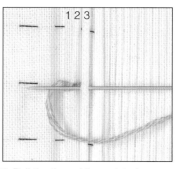

3. Pull the thread through to form an under cable. With the thread still below and the needle horizontal, take it from right to left through the third pleat.

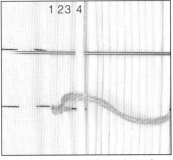

4. Pull the thread through to form another cable. Wave up to the next row and take a stitch through the fourth pleat.

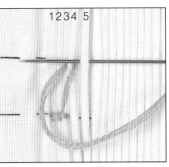

5. Pull the thread through. With the thread below, take a stitch through the fifth pleat.

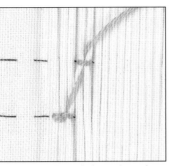

6. Pull the thread through to form another cable.

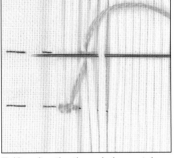

7. Keeping the thread above, take a stitch through the next pleat.

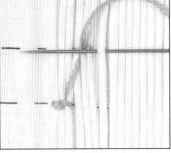

8. Pull the thread through to form another cable. With the thread above, take a stitch through the next pleat.

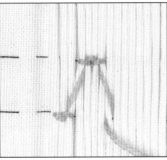

9. Pull the thread through. With the thread above, wave down to the next row and take a stitch through the next pleat.

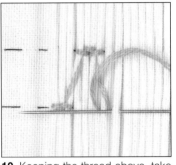

10. Keeping the thread above, take a stitch through the next pleat.

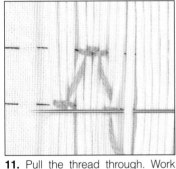

11. Pull the thread through. Work another cable. Keeping the thread below, take a stitch through the next pleat.

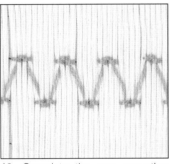

12. Complete the row, repeating steps 3 - 10.

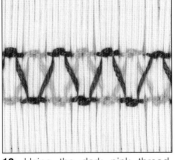

13. Using the dark pink thread, stitch a second row, using the free pleats between the stitches of the first row.

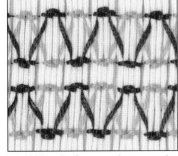

14. With a half-space between the first rows and the second, work mirror image rows in the same thread sequence.

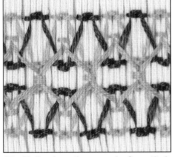

15. Following the graph for stitch placement, work rows of wave over the previous stitching, using the orange thread.

Color Key

DMC perlé 8 cotton

A = 603 cranberry
B = 703 lt Kelly green
C = 741 med tangerine
D = 972 deep canary
E = 3348 lt yellow-green

Embroidery Key

*All embroidery is worked with
one strand of thread.*

Blush pink flowers = C or D
(straight stitch) and A (cross stitch)
Rose pink flowers = C (cross stitch
and colonial knot)
Gold flowers = C (straight stitch)
Aqua flowers = D (cross stitch)
Scrolls = B (back stitch)
Leaves = E (back stitch)

The bag measures 8 ¼" wide x 10 ¼" high (21cm x 26cm)

Bag

Requirements

Fabric

13 ¾" x 59" wide (35cm x 150cm) dark taupe heavyweight cotton

10" x 59" wide (25cm x 150cm) floral cotton print

Notions

Blush pink, rose pink, gold and aqua felt

4 ¾" (12cm) square of each

13 ¾" x 43 ¼" wide (35cm x 110cm) heavyweight interfacing

10" x 11 ¾" wide (25cm x 30cm) transparent acetate

Fine tip permanent marker

Chalk-based fabric marker

Scalpel (or similar sharp bladed cutting knife)

No. 6 crewel needle (embroidery)

Threads

See opposite page.

Cutting out

See the liftout pattern sheet for the cutting layouts.

Dark taupe heavyweight cotton

Bag front: cut one, 9" x 11" wide (23cm x 28cm)

Cut out the remaining pieces following the instructions on the pattern sheet.

Preparation for Embroidery

See the pattern sheet for the embroidery design and flower templates.

Stylized flowers, cut from brightly colored felt and attached with simple embroidery stitches, form the basis of this design.

Transferring the design

Cut a 4" (10cm) strip from one edge of the acetate. Trace the flower shapes onto this strip with the permanent marker and cut out to use as templates.

Lay the larger piece of acetate over the design and trace the placement marks, scrolls, leaves and positions of the flowers with the permanent marker. Pierce holes at the positions for the flowers with a skewer or similar tool. Using the scalpel, cut narrow channels in the acetate on the scrolls and cut out the leaf shapes.

Place this template over the front, matching the placement marks. Using the chalk based marker, trace the design lines and flower placement marks onto the fabric through the holes and channels in the acetate.

Cutting out the flowers

Tracing around the templates with the fabric marker, mark one large and one small flower on the blush pink felt. Cut just inside the marked lines. Cut two flowers from the rose pink and the gold felt, and three flowers from the aqua felt, in the same manner.

Cut two circles, one ⅜" (10mm) and the other ½" (13mm) from the blue felt and a ½" (13mm) circle from the gold felt for the flower centers.

Embroidery

See the opposite page for the embroidery key.

Embroider the scrolls and leaves, using back stitch.

Pink flowers

Pin the large blush pink flower in position. Using the pink thread, work a cross stitch at the end of each petal to secure the flower. Position the gold felt circle in the center. Work pairs of straight stitches at the 12, 4, 6 and 9 o'clock positions to attach the center.

Pin the small blush pink flower in position. Using pairs of straight stitches that radiate from a space in the center and extend a short distance up each petal, stitch the flower to the bag.

Attach both the rose pink flowers with a colonial knot at the end of each petal and a cross stitch in the center using the orange thread.

Gold flowers

Pin the large gold flower in position. Place the large blue circle slightly off center on the flower. Attach the flower with pairs of straight stitches at the 12, 2, 4, 7 and 9 o'clock positions using the yellow thread.

Attach the small yellow flower in the same manner, using the small blue circle in the center.

Aqua flowers

Attach the aqua flowers with a cross stitch in the center. Work two stitches for each section of the cross.

Construction

See page 113.

Cute as a button in soft denim

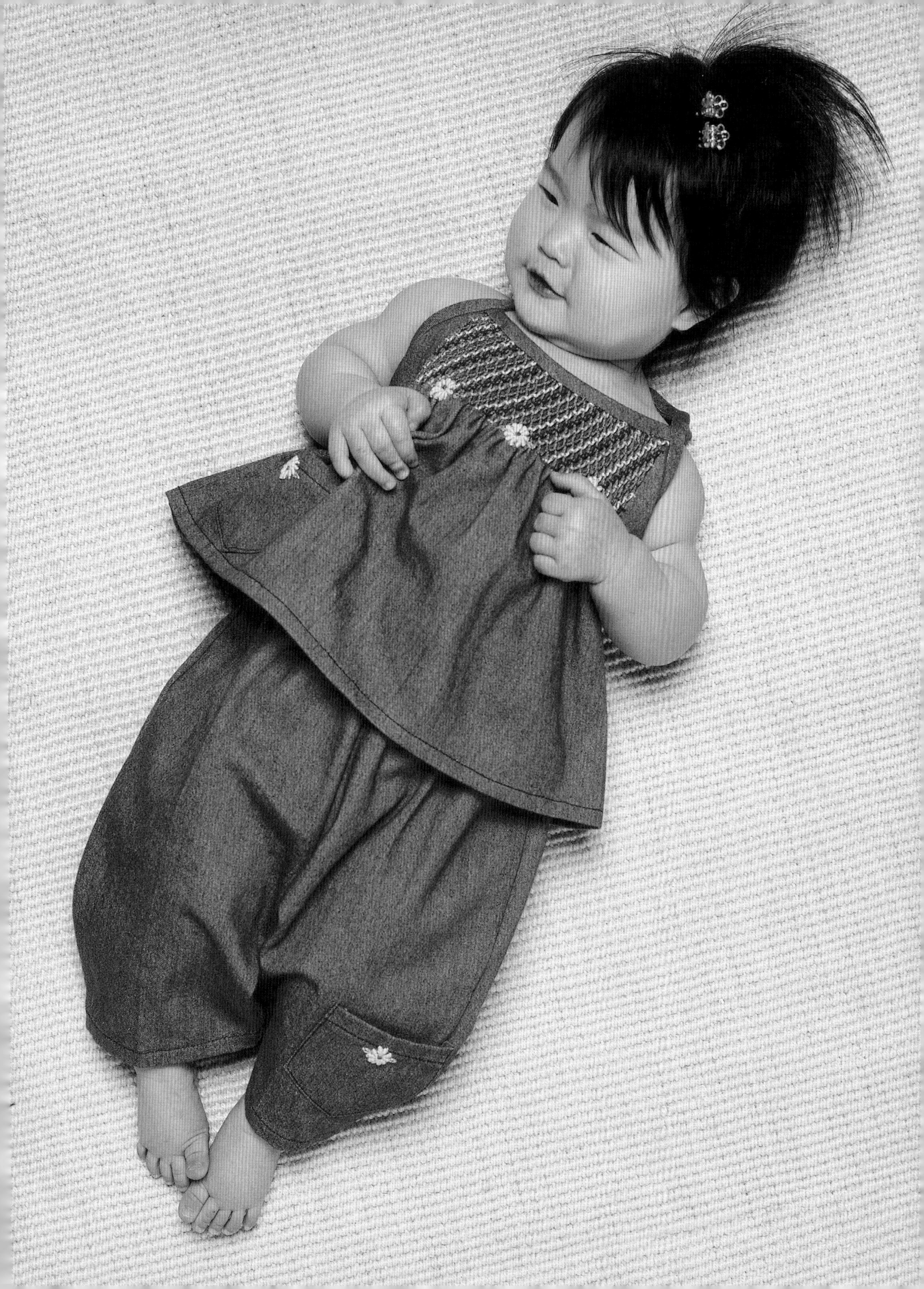

Trendy Tot

By **Merrilin Wilder**

This cool and practical outfit will take your little one from playgroup to a Wiggles concert in style.

Denim fabric, highlighted with vibrant red top-stitching and cheerful embroidered daisy motifs, perfectly complements the colorful smocking.

Requirements for top and pants

Sizes 6, 12 and 24 months

Fabric

Lightweight blue denim 44" (112cm) wide
Size 6 months: 39 ⅜" (1m)
Size 12 months: 43 ¼" (1.1m)
Size 24 months: 47 ¾" (1.2m)

Notions

Red machine topstitching thread
18" x ¾" wide (46cm x 20mm) white non-roll elastic
7" x ⁵⁄₁₆" (18cm x 7mm) white elastic
No. 5 crewel needle (smocking)
No. 3 milliner's needle (embroidery)

Threads

See page 76.

Pattern

See the liftout pattern sheet.

We recommend that you read the complete article and the pattern instructions relating to this project before you begin.

The finished back length of the top is
Size 6 months: 6 ½" (16.5cm)
Size 12 months: 7 ⅝" (19.5cm)
Size 24 months: 8 ½" (21.5cm)
The finished length of the pants at the side is
Size 6 months: 13 ⅜" (34cm)
Size 12 months: 15" (38cm)
Size 24 months: 16 ½" (42cm)
There is no hem allowance on either garment.

Cutting Out

See the liftout pattern sheet for the cutting layout.

Lightweight blue denim

Front: cut one
Size 6 months: 10 ⅝" x 21 ⅝" wide (27cm x 55cm)
Size 12 months: 11 ¾" x 22 ½" wide (30cm x 57cm)
Size 24 months: 13" x 23 ¼" wide (33cm x 59cm)
Note: the neckline and armhole shaping will be cut after the front has been pleated and smocked.

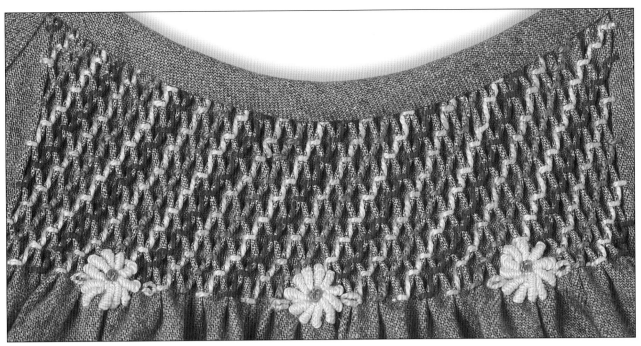

Front

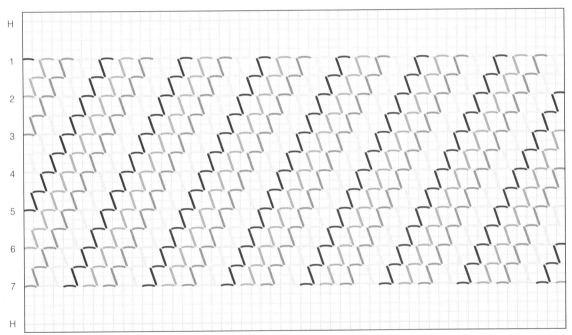

Trace the pattern pieces onto lightweight interfacing or tracing paper, transferring the pattern markings. Cut out all the remaining pieces following the instructions on the pattern sheet.

Preparation & Pleating

Pleat 9 full space rows (including two holding rows) with the top row ⅜" (1cm) from the upper raw edge.

This design uses 56 pleats for all sizes. Count the pleats and mark the center valley. Leaving 28 pleats on both sides of the center valley, unpick the pleating threads at the sides. Tie off so that the pleated area measures 5 ½" (14cm).

Hint

Thoroughly prewash the denim fabric to remove the excess dye. This should prevent the pale thread colors becoming stained with the blue dye as you work.

Smocking

See the step-by-step instructions for stepped Van Dyke stitch on page 87. Refer to the graph and color key for thread color changes.

The smocking is worked from right to left.

Row 1 - 7. Using the pale yellow thread and beginning on the last two pleats on the right hand side on row 1 with an over cable, work stepped Van Dyke stitch down to row 7.

Changing thread color for each row, repeat row 1 - 7 until all the pleats have been covered.

Referring to the graph for exact stitch placement and maintaining color sequence, fill in the remaining rows on the right hand side of the design.

Embroidery

See this page for the embroidery key.

See the opposite page for step-by-step instructions for bullion knot daisy.

Top

We recommend that you remove the pleating threads except for the top holding row before working the embroidery on the smocking. Construct the top following the instructions on pages 113 - 115 before working the embroidery on the pockets.

Embroidery on the smocking

Work the middle daisy at the center two pleats between rows 6 ½ and 7 ½. Embroider 11 bullion knots for the petals using D and stitch a French knot for the center using B. Work a detached chain leaf at each side using C. Embroider the remaining two daisies at the lower edge of the smocking in the same manner, referring to the close-up photograph for placement.

Pocket

Embroider a single daisy at the center of the upper edge of the pocket, just below the topstitched seamline in the same manner as the daisies on the smocking.

Pants

Pocket

Embroider a single daisy on the pocket in the same manner as the top at the marked position on the pattern piece.

Construction

See pages 113 - 115.

Color Key

DMC no. 5 perlé cotton
A = 321 vy lt garnet
B = 351 coral
C = 3348 lt yellow-green
D = 3823 ultra lt yellow
Smocking = A, B, C and D
(1 strand)
Embroidery = B, C and D

Embroidery Key

All embroidery is worked with one strand.

Daisy

Center = B
(French knot
two wraps)

Petals = D (11 bullion knots
10 wraps)
Leaves = C (detached chain)

76

The wraps in each bullion knot of this daisy have been manipulated to be loose on the outer edge and tight in the center. There are eleven bullion knots spaced evenly around a central point and a French knot in the center.

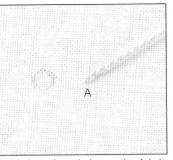

1. Mark a tiny circle on the fabric approximately ⅛" (2-3mm). Bring the thread to the front at A ¼" (6mm) away from the circle.

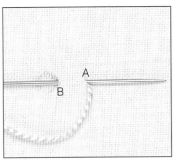

2. Take the needle to the back at B and re-emerge at A.

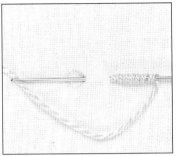

3. Wrap the thread around the needle ten times.

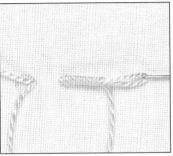

4. Begin to pull the thread through the wraps, keeping a firm tension with your thumb.

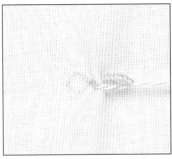

5. Continuing to keep the tension on the wraps, pull the thread through until a pleat forms in the fabric.

6. Smooth out the fabric. Give the knot a gentle tug and let the wraps wind down at the end. Keep the outer wraps slightly larger than the inner wraps.

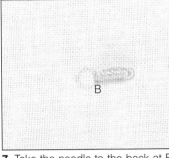

7. Take the needle to the back at B and pull the thread through.

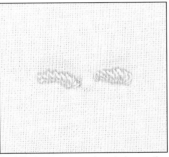

8. Work a second petal on the opposite side of the circle in the same manner as before.

9. Work four more petals below, spacing them evenly between the first two.

10. Work five petals above as before. Work a French knot at the center and a detached chain leaf on each side of the petals.

Stitch Book

When working a row of cable, always keep the needle horizontal for each stitch and in the same position on the pleating row. The needle position does not change at all - only the thread position. When you work an under cable, the thread is below the needle. Give a gentle tug in a downward direction to position the thread for the next stitch. When working an over cable, the thread is above the needle. Tug the thread in an upward direction.

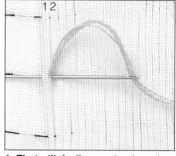

1. First stitch. Secure the thread on the back. Bring it to the front between pleats 1 and 2. Take the needle from right to left through the first pleat.

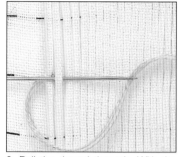

2. Pull the thread through. With the thread below, take the needle through the next pleat, on top of the pleating thread. This will form an under cable.

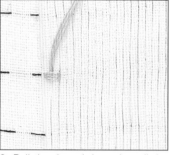

3. Pull the thread through until the stitch is snug against the pleats. Gently tug downwards to reposition the thread for the next stitch.

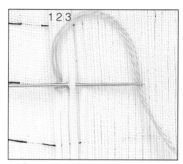

4. Second stitch. With the thread above the needle, take the needle through pleat 3. This will form an over cable.

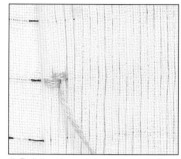

5. Pull the thread through as before. Gently tug upwards to reposition the thread for the next stitch.

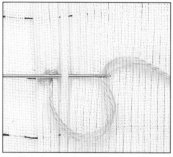

6. Third stitch. With the thread below, take the needle through the next pleat for the second under cable.

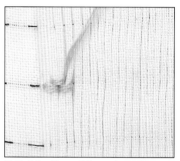

7. Pull the thread through and tug as in step 3.

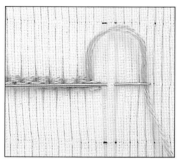

8. Continue across the row, alternating the thread position, keeping the needle horizontal and on top of the pleating row for each stitch.

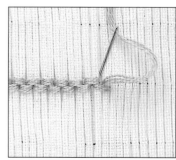

9. Take the needle to the back of the fabric through the valley in the middle of this last stitch.

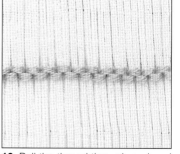

10. Pull the thread through and end off the thread on the back of the fabric.

The stitches on the second row should just touch the stitches on the first row.
An over cable on the second row will 'kiss' the under cable on the row above. Double cable can be worked using the same color thread or contrasting threads, forming a thick bold border.

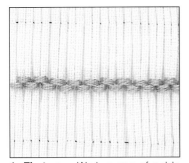

1. First row. Work a row of cable following the instructions for single cable stitch.

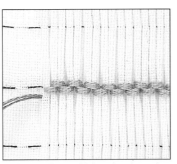

2. Second row. Bring the thread to the front a needle's width below the first cable of the first row.

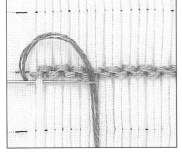

3. With the thread above the needle, take the needle through the second pleat.

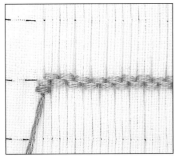

4. Pull the thread through and gently tug upwards. This over cable will just touch the under cable on the row above.

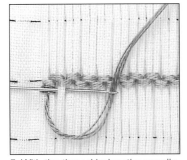

5. With the thread below the needle, take the needle through the third pleat.

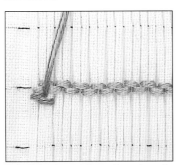

6. Pull the thread through and gently tug downwards.

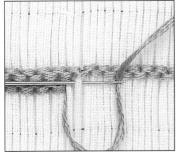

7. Continue, alternating the thread position for each stitch but keeping the needle horizontal and exactly the same distance from the first row.

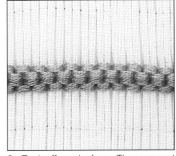

8. End off as before. The second row is a mirror image of the first row.

Alternating cable or cable picot is an attractive stitch which can be worked in a single color or two colors. Each gives a very different effect.

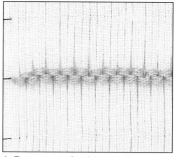

1. Base row of cable. Work a row of cable following the instructions for single cable stitch.

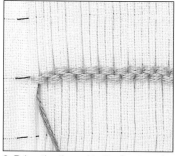

2. Bring the thread to the front on the right hand side of the first pleat, a needle's width below the first stitch of the base row.

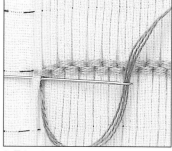

3. Take the needle back through the first pleat from right to left.

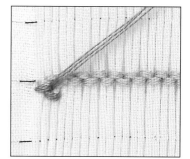

4. Pull the thread through. Work two cables (an over cable then an under cable).

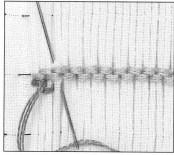

5. Keep the thread below the needle and angle it to emerge on the left side of the same pleat, a needle's width above the base row.

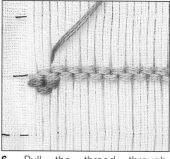

6. Pull the thread through. Completed first picot.

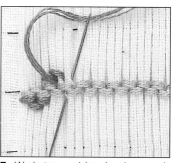

7. Work two cables (under, over). With thread above, take the needle through next pleat angling it to emerge below the base row.

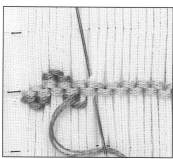

8. Pull the thread through. Work two cables (over, under). For the next cable, angle the needle through the pleat. Emerge above the base cable row as in step 5.

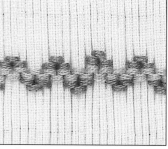

9. Continue, alternating between three cables below the base row and three above. End off the thread.

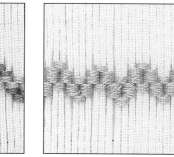

10. Alternating cable worked with a single color.

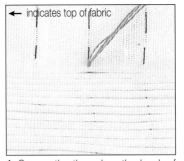

1. Secure the thread on the back of the fabric on the right hand side. Bring it to the front on the upper side of pleat 1 on the pleating row.

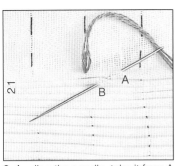

2. Angling the needle, take it from A to B through pleats 1 and 2. A is two thirds of the way to the next pleating row and B is one third of the way.

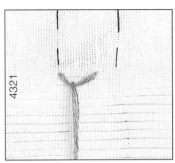

3. Loop the thread to the right ensuring it is under the tip of the needle.

Feather stitch is worked from right to left and is often easier to work while holding the fabric sideways as shown here. The important thing is to keep the spacing consistent.

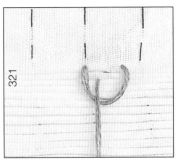

4. Keeping constant tension on the thread, pull it through with a downward movement.

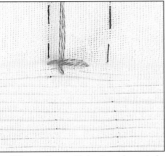

5. When the stitch is almost in position, give a slight tug away from you. This ensures even tension and a nicely shaped stitch.

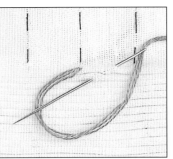

6. Still holding the thread, pull it towards you. This action helps to settle the stitch in position on the pleats.

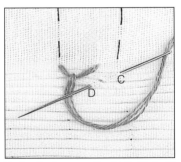

7. Angle the needle from C to D through pleats 2 and 3. D is a one third space to the left of C. Loop the thread to the right under the tip of the needle.

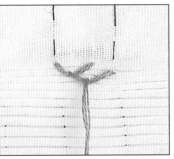

8. Pull the thread through and settle the stitch as before.

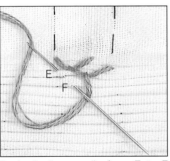

9. Angle the needle from E to F through pleats 3 and 4. F is a one third space to the right of E. Loop the thread to the left under the tip of the needle.

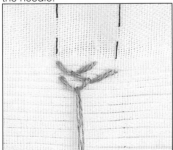

10. Pull the thread through and settle the stitch as before.

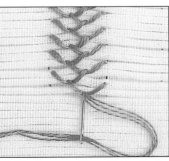

11. Continue working stitches in the same manner. After the last stitch, take the needle to the back of the fabric on the lower side of the last used pleat.

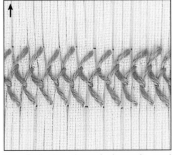

12. Pull the thread through and secure on the back of the fabric.

Also known as chevron stitch, wave stitch is one of the most commonly used smocking stitches. It forms the basis of many designs and is easy to combine with other stitches.

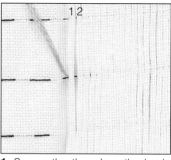

1. Secure the thread on the back. Bring it to the front between pleats 1 and 2. Take it from right to left through pleat 1.

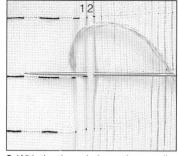

2. With the thread above the needle, take the needle from right to left through pleat 2.

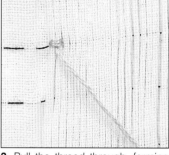

3. Pull the thread through, forming an over cable.

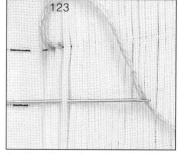

4. Keeping the thread above and the needle horizontal, take it from right to left through pleat 3 on the pleating row below.

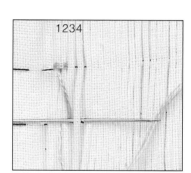

5. Pull the thread through. With the thread below the needle, take the needle from right to left through pleat 4.

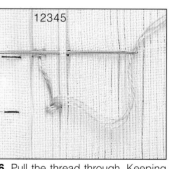

6. Pull the thread through. Keeping the thread below, take the needle from right to left through pleat 5 on the upper pleating row.

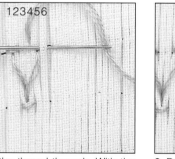

7. Pull the thread through. With the thread above the needle, take it from right to left through pleat 6.

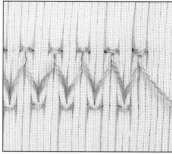

8. Pull the thread through. Continue in the same manner across the row, ending with a cable stitch.

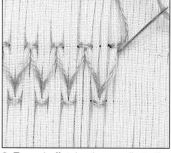

9. To end off, take the needle to the back of the fabric through the valley of the last stitch.

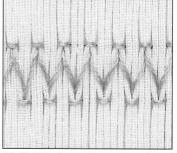

10. Pull the thread through and end off the thread on the back of the fabric.

Wave stitch diamonds form when every following row is a mirror image of the previous row. They can be worked using either half space or full space wave stitches. Here we show half space wave diamonds.

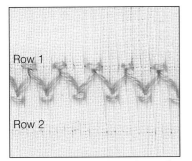

1. First row. Following the instructions for full space wave, work a row of wave stitches between row 1 - 1 ½.

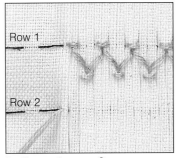

2. Second row. Secure a new thread and bring it to the front on row 2.

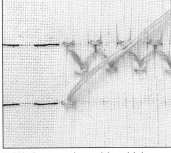

3. Work an under cable which uses the same two pleats as the first over cable in the previous row.

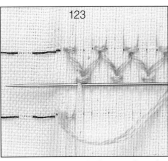

4. With thread below, take the needle from right to left through pleat 3, just below the under cable of the previous row.

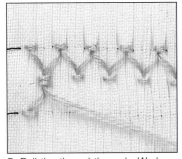

5. Pull the thread through. Work an over cable directly below the cable of the previous row.

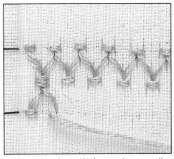

6. With the thread above the needle, work a wave stitch down to the pleating row below.

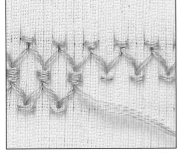

7. Continue across the row, ensuring the over cables lie directly below the under cables of the previous row.

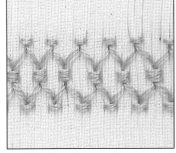

8. Pull the thread through and secure on the back of the fabric.

Van Dyke stitch is one of the oldest smocking stitches and is a very strong, secure, elastic stitch. Work from right to left, picking up two pleats for each stitch, one 'old' pleat and one 'new' pleat.

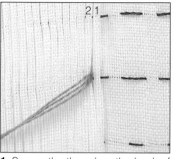

1. Secure the thread on the back of the fabric on the right hand side. Bring it to the front between pleats 1 and 2 on the upper pleating row.

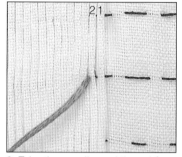

2. Take the needle and thread from right to left through pleat 2 ready to begin stitching.

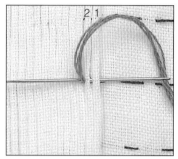

3. With the thread above the needle, take the needle from right to left through pleats 1 and 2.

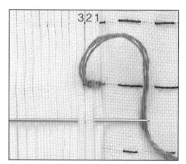

4. Pull the thread through. Keeping the thread above, take the needle from right to left through pleats 2 and 3 halfway to the next pleating row.

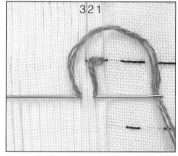

5. Pull the thread through. Still keeping the thread above, take the needle from right to left through pleats 2 and 3 again.

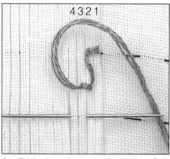

6. Pull the thread through. Still keeping the thread above, take the needle from right to left through pleats 3 and 4 on the pleating row below.

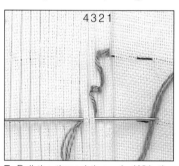

7. Pull the thread through. With the thread below, take the needle from right to left through pleats 3 and 4 again.

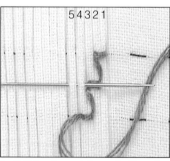

8. Pull the thread through. Keeping the thread below, take the needle from right to left through pleats 4 and 5 on the half space above.

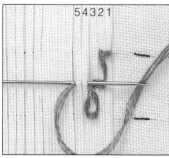

9. Pull the thread through. Keeping the thread below, take the needle from right to left through pleats 4 and 5 again.

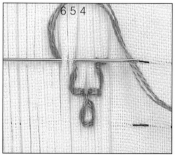

10. Take a stitch through pleats 5 and 6 on the upper row. Take the needle through the same pleats to complete the second stitch.

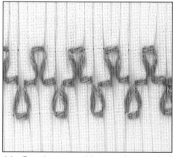

11. Continue working to the end of the row in the same manner.

As Van Dyke stitch is extremely elastic, this example will often require backsmocking to prevent the work from becoming too stretched.

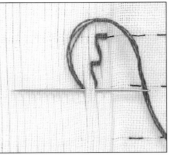

1. Work steps 1 - 7 for double Van Dyke stitch.

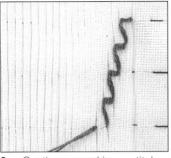

2. Continue working stitches downwards in the same manner for the required distance.

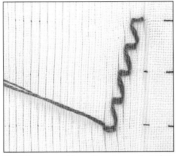

3. After reaching the lowest point, take the thread below the needle and work a horizontal stitch through the last two pleats used.

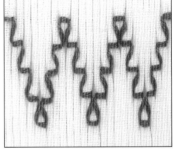

4. Keeping the thread below, work Van Dyke stitch up to the top. Continue across the row.

The rows in this design are worked close together creating an interesting texture of diagonal stripes. This will also ensure the panel will not become over stretched.

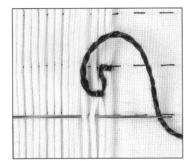

1. Work steps 1-6 for double Van Dyke stitch.

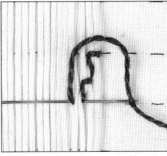

2. Pull the thread through. Keeping the thread above, take the needle from right to left through pleats 3 and 4 again.

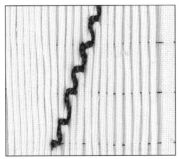

3. Continue working stepped Van Dyke stitch in the same manner down to row 7. Take the thread to the back through the valley to left of the last two pleats used on row 7.

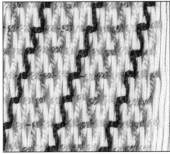

4. Following the graph for thread colors and stitch placement, continue for the required number of rows.

Bullion Rose

This classic rose is created from two rounds of bullion knot petals surrounding a pair of bullion knots. Roses of various sizes can be made by changing the number of strands or wraps and the size of the needle.

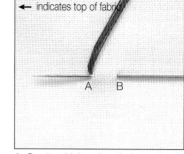

1. Center. Using the darkest shade of thread, bring it to the front at A. Take the needle from B to A, taking care not to split the thread.

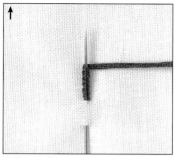

2. Rotate fabric so the needle points away from you. Raise the tip and wrap the thread clockwise around the needle the required number of times.

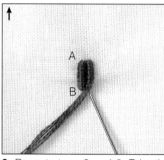

3. Keeping tension on the wraps with the left thumb, pull the thread through.

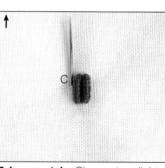

4. Pull the knot towards B. Take the needle to the back at B and pull the thread through. Bring the needle to the front very close to A.

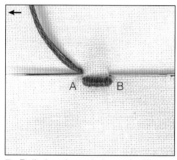

5. Pull the thread through. Rotate the fabric. Take the needle from B to A, keeping the thread above the needle.

6. Repeat steps 2 and 3. Take the needle to the back at B to anchor the second bullion knot.

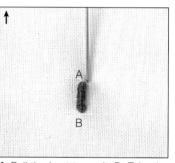

7. Inner petals. Change to a lighter shade of thread. Bring the needle to the front at C.

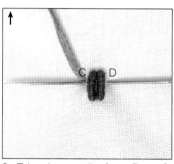

8. Take the needle from D to C, keeping the thread above the needle.

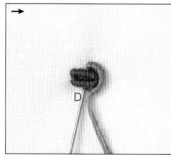

9. Repeat steps 2 and 3 with the required number of wraps. Settle the knot. Take the needle to the back at D to anchor the knot.

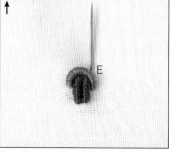

10. Rotate the fabric. Bring the needle to the front at E.

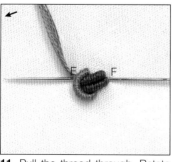

11. Pull the thread through. Rotate the fabric slightly. Take the needle from F to E.

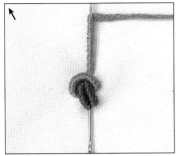

12. Rotate the fabric. Place the required number of wraps on the needle, holding the thread taut to maintain tension on the wraps.

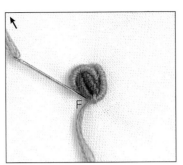

13. Take the needle to the back at F to anchor the knot.

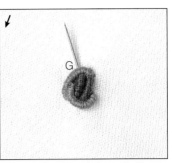

14. Pull the thread through. Rotate the fabric. Bring the needle to the front at G.

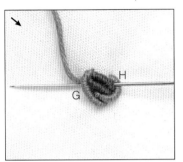

15. Pull the thread through. Rotate the fabric. Take the needle from H (inside the first petal) to G.

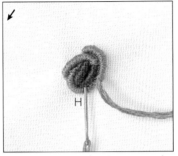

16. Rotate the fabric, wrap the needle and pull thread through. Adjust the stitch. Take needle to the back at H, inside the first inner petal.

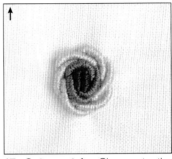

17. Outer petals. Change to the lightest thread. Work the required number of petals in a similar manner to form the third round.

Bullion Loop

A bullion loop is formed in a similar manner to a bullion knot except that the distance between A and B is quite small and the number of wraps is large.

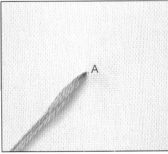

1. Bring the needle to the front at A. Pull the thread through.

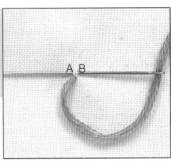

2. Take the needle through the fabric from B to A, taking care not to split the thread. The thread is below the needle.

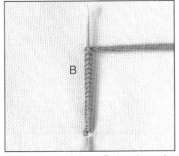

3. Rotate the fabric. Raise the point of the needle and wrap the thread around it the required number of times.

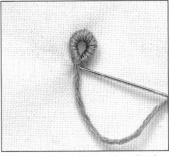

4. Pull the thread through, adjusting the wraps. Take the needle to the back at B to anchor the loop.

Trellis stitch is a very elastic stitch and is formed by working a combination of cable and stepped stitches.

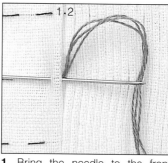

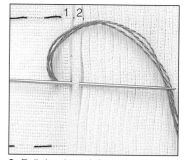

1. Bring the needle to the front between pleats 1 and 2. Take the needle from right to left through pleat 1 ready to begin stitching.

2. Pull the thread through. With the thread above the needle, take the needle from right to left through pleat 2.

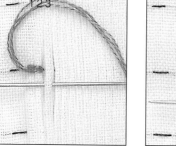

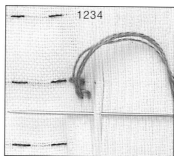

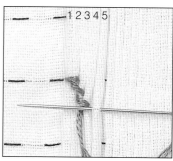

3. Pull the thread through. Keeping the thread above and the needle horizontal, take it from right to left through pleat 3 a quarter space below.

4. Pull the thread through. Keeping the thread above and the needle horizontal, take it from right to left through pleat 4, a quarter space below.

5. Pull the thread through. With the thread below the needle and still on the half space, take the needle from right to left through pleat 5.

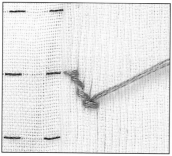

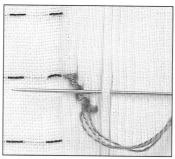

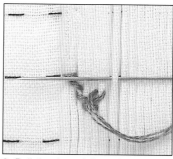

6. Pull the thread through to form a cable stitch.

7. Keeping the thread below the needle, take the needle from right to left through the next pleat a quarter space above.

8. Pull the thread through. Keeping the thread below the needle, take the needle from right to left through the next pleat on the pleating row above.

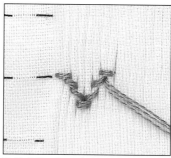

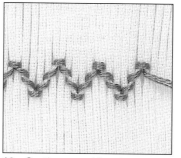

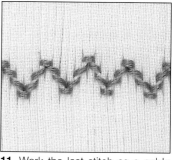

9. Pull the thread through. Work an over cable on the pleating row.

10. Continue working two steps down, under cable, two steps up, over cable across the row.

11. Work the last stitch as a cable stitch. Take the thread to the back of the fabric in the valley of the last stitch and end off.

Outline stitch looks best when worked with a firm, even tension. It is easier to keep the stitching straight along a pleating row. The first few stitches may appear to slope. Your smocking is not crooked, it is the stitches skewing the fabric. Keep stitching and the line will straighten out.

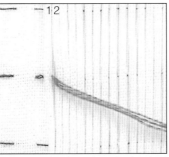

1. Secure the thread on the back of the fabric. Bring it to the front between pleats 1 and 2.

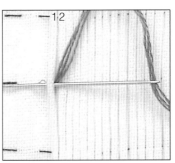

2. Take the needle from right to left through pleat 1. Pull the thread through ready to begin stitching.

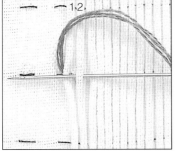

3. With the thread above the needle and the needle horizontal, take it from right to left through pleat 2.

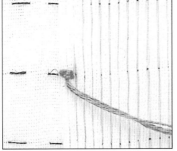

4. Pull the thread through until the stitch sits snug against the pleat.

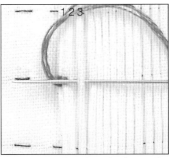

5. Keeping the thread above the needle, take the needle from right to left through pleat 3.

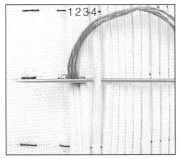

6. Pull the thread through as before. Keeping the thread above the needle, take the needle from right to left through pleat 4.

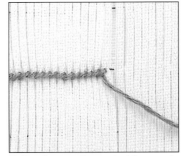

7. Continue to the end of the row in the same manner.

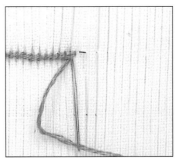

8. To end off, take the needle and thread to the back of the fabric through the valley just below the last outline stitch.

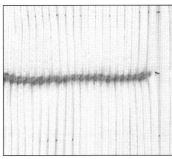

9. Pull the thread through and secure on the back of the fabric.

Construction

General Instructions

1. Cutting out

Trace the pattern pieces onto light-weight interfacing or tracing paper, transferring the pattern markings. Where pattern pieces are not provided, cut the pieces according to the measurements given. Cut out all pieces following the appropriate cutting layouts.

2. Blocking the smocking

Remove the pleating threads except for the top holding row. With the right side uppermost, place the smocking onto a padded surface such as an ironing board. Pin to fit the appropriate blocking guide or the given measurement, ensuring the smocking is straight and even. Steam, ensuring the iron does not touch the smocking. Alternatively, dampen by spraying with a water atomiser. Leave pinned until dry.

3. Seams

Flat seam

With right sides together and matching raw edges, pin and stitch the pieces of fabric together using the appropriate seam allowance. Trim the seam if necessary and neaten the raw edges with a narrow zigzag or machine overlock stitch *(diag 1)*. Press.

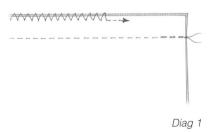

Diag 1

French seam

Pin the pieces with wrong sides together. Stitch ¼" (6mm) from the raw edge. Trim the seam to ⅛" (3mm) *(diag 2)*.

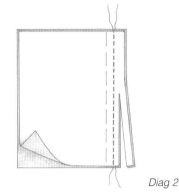

Diag 2

Bringing the right sides together, fold the fabric along the seam and press. Stitch again, enclosing the raw edges *(diag 3)*. Press.

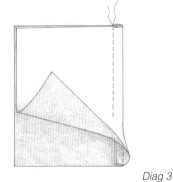

Diag 3

4. Elastic casing for pants

Cut a length of the non-roll elastic to fit around the child's waist plus ¾" (2cm) to overlap the ends.

Alternatively, cut a length the following measurement.

Size newborn: 14 ¾" (37.5cm)
Size 3 months: 15 ½" (39.5cm)
Size 6 months: 16 ⅜" (41.5cm)
Size 1: 17 ⅛" (43.5cm)
Size 2: 17 ⅞" (45.5cm)
Size 3: 18 ¼" (46.5cm)
Size 4: 18 ⅝" (47.5cm)
Size 8: 19 ⅞" (50.5cm)
Size 10: 20 ⅝" (52.5cm)
Size 12: 21 ½" (54.5cm)

The measurements above are given as a guide only.

Fold under ¼" (5mm) along the upper edge of the pants and press.

Fold under a further 1" (2.5cm) and press. Pin and stitch close to the folded edge to form a casing, leaving a 2" (5cm) opening at the center back *(diag 4)*.

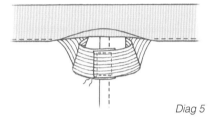

Diag 4

Thread the elastic through the casing and stitch the ends securely *(diag 5)*.

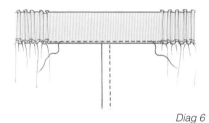

Diag 5

Stitch the opening in the casing closed *(diag 6)*.

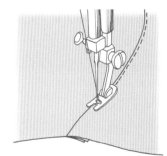

Diag 6

5. Topstitching

Stitch the seam, neaten and press following the instructions given for that particular part of the garment.

Machine stitch on the right side along the fold of the seam, through all layers *(diag 7)*.

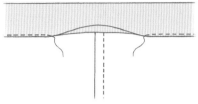

Diag 7

Note: The shading on the diagrams throughout this section indicates the right side of the fabric.

Golden Sands

*For color photos and full details
see pages 6 - 13*

Sizes 8, 10, 12 and 14 years

TOP FRONT   TOP BACK

SKIRT FRONT   SKIRT BACK

REQUIREMENTS

For full details, see pages 8 and 12.

CUTTING OUT

See the liftout pattern sheet.

PREPARATION & PLEATING

For full instructions, see page 9.

SMOCKING & EMBROIDERY

For full instructions, see pages 9 - 13.

CONSTRUCTION

*All seam allowances are ⅜" (1cm)
unless otherwise specified.*

TOP

1. Shaping the smocking

Cut out the marked armhole shaping,
leaving the upper holding row in place.

2. Binding the upper edge of the front

Neaten one long edge of the binding
strip with a machine zigzag or overlock
stitch. With right sides together,
matching raw edges and slightly
stretching the binding, pin the binding to
the right side of the front, aligning the
stitchline just above the first row of
smocking. Stitch (*diag 1*).

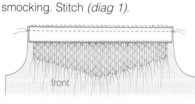

front

Diag 1

Stitch again ⁵⁄₁₆" (7mm) away within the
seam allowance. Trim close to the
second line of stitching. Fold the
binding to the wrong side and pin.
Topstitch close to the seam on the right
side, securing the other edge of the
binding on the wrong side (*diag 2*).

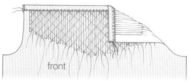

front

Diag 2

3. Binding the upper edge of the back

Stitch two rows of machine gathering
across the upper edge of the back. Pull
up the gathers to measure ⅝" (1.5cm)
more than the length of the back binding
and secure. Attach the binding in the
same manner as the front.

4. Side seams

With right sides
together, pin and stitch
the front to the back at
the sides (*diag 3*).

Trim and neaten the
seams. Press towards
the back. Neaten the
lower edge of the top
with an overlock stitch.

Clip the side
seams 1" (2.5cm)
from the lower
edge and press
this section of the
seam to the front
(*diag 4*).

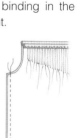

Diag 3

Diag 4

5. Straps and armhole binding

Neaten one long edge of both binding
strips with an overlock stitch. With right
sides together and matching raw
edges, stitch the short ends of the
binding together to form a circle (*diag 5*).
Press the seams open.

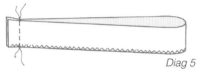

Diag 5

With right sides together, matching
seams and slightly stretching the
binding, pin the binding to one armhole
edge. Stitch (*diag 6*).

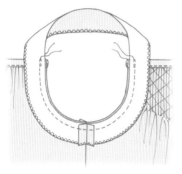

Diag 6

Fold the binding over the seam to the
wrong side, ensuring the neatened
edge of the binding just conceals the
previous row of
stitching on the
armhole edges
and the
neatened edge
doesn't show
on the right
side of the
strap section
(*diag 7*).
Pin in place.
Topstitch close
to the seam on
the right side,
securing the
neatened edge
of the binding
on the wrong
side in the
armhole
sections and

back

Diag 7

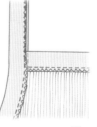

Diag 8

just catching the neatened edge on the
strap section (*diag 8*).

6. Elastic casing

Neaten the lower edge of the top with an overlock stitch. Press under 1" (2.5cm) along the lower edge and tack in place. On the wrong side, rule a line around the top ¾" (2cm) away from the neatened edge of the hem.

Handstitch one end of the length of elastic to the side seam just above the hem edge. Using a blind hemming stitch on the widest setting and a short stitch length, stitch over the elastic, securing the hem at the same time (diag 9).

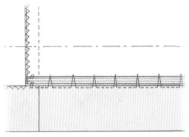

Diag 9

Do not catch the elastic in the stitching or stretch it too much at this stage. At the beginning, cut the length of elastic, leaving a 2" (5cm) tail. Stitching from the other direction and placing the straight stitches along the marked line, attach another row of elastic in the same manner (diag 10).

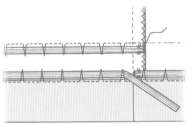

Diag 10

Pull on the tails of elastic one at a time, gathering the casing to measure

Size 8: 17" (43cm)

Size 10: 17 ¾" (45cm)

Size 12: 18 ½" (47cm)

Size 14: 19 ¼" (49cm)

Trim off the excess elastic leaving a short overlap and handstitch the ends of elastic together to secure.

Work the herringbone stitching over the casing following the instructions on pages 10 and 13.

SKIRT

All seam allowances are ⅝" (1.5cm) unless otherwise specified.

1. Side seams

With right sides together and matching the rows of smocking, stitch the skirt pieces together on one side (diag 11).

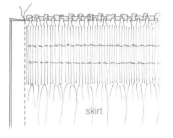

Diag 11

Neaten both sides of the seam separately and press open. Repeat for the remaining side, leaving a 4 ⅛" (10.5cm) opening at the top. This will be the left hand side seam.

2. Ties

Matching raw edges, fold the ties in half along the length. Stitch down the long edge and across one end using a ¼" (6mm) seam allowance (diag 12).

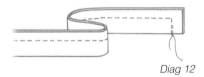

Diag 12

Clip the corners at the stitched narrow end and turn the tie through to the right side. Press.

With the seam positioned downwards, baste the raw end of a tie 1" (2.5cm) down from the upper raw edge on both sides of one front yoke (diag 13).

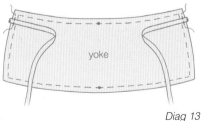

Diag 13

3. Waist band

With right sides together, pin and stitch one back yoke to the left hand side of the yoke with the ties attached (diag 14). Press the seam open.

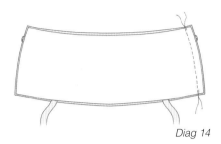

Diag 14

Stitch the remaining band pieces together in the same manner. This will be the yoke lining.

With right sides together, matching side seams and placing the stitchline on the yoke just above the first row of smocking, pin and stitch the lower edge of the yoke to the upper edge of the skirt (diag 15).

Diag 15

Trim and neaten the seam. Press the yoke away from the skirt.

4. Invisible zipper

Using the appropriate foot and the manufacturer's instructions, insert the invisible zipper into the opening in the side seam (diag 16). Open the zipper.

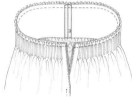

Diag 16

5. Yoke lining

With right sides together and matching the seams, pin and stitch the yoke lining to the yoke along the top edge (diag 17).

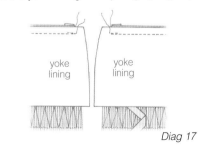

Diag 17

The lining will extend ⅝" (1.5cm) past the zipper at the opening. Press under the seam allowance on the lower edge of the lining and trim to ⅜" (1cm). Fold under slightly more than the seam allowance at the sides and pin, aligning the fold with the zipper stitching. Matching the side seams, pin the lower edge to align with the stitchline securing the yoke to the skirt. Handstitch down the sides of the zipper and along the lower edge (diag 18).

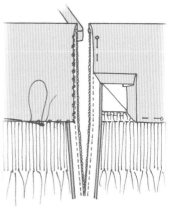

Diag 18

6. Hemline

Tuck

Press under 5 ¾" (14.5cm) along the lower edge of the skirt. Stitch a ¾" (2cm) tuck. Press the tuck downwards.

Hem

Neaten the lower edge of the skirt with a machine zigzag or overlock stitch. Press under a ¾" (2cm) hem and machine stitch close to the neatened edge. Press.

7. Finishing

Stitch the hook and eye in place above the zipper. Work the crocheted edge along the lower edge of the tuck and the hem following the instructions on page 12. Tie a knot in the end of each tie.

For color photos and full details see pages 26 - 29

Sizes 6, 8 and 10 years

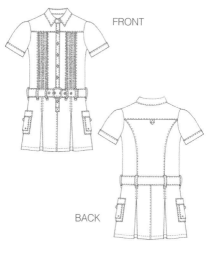

FRONT

BACK

REQUIREMENTS

For full details, see page 28 and 29.

CUTTING OUT

See the liftout pattern sheet.

PLEATING

For full instructions, see page 29.

SMOCKING

For full instructions, see page 29.

CONSTRUCTION

All seam allowances are ⅜" (1cm) unless otherwise specified.

Note: topstitch ⅛" (2 - 3mm) away from the fold.

1. Blocking and shaping the smocking

Block the smocking following the instructions on page 92, leaving the holding rows in place. Place an insert lining piece on the wrong side of each

insert, aligning the long edges with the holding rows. Baste in place (diag 1).

insert lining

Diag 1

Trim the edges of the smocked inserts level with the linings.

2. Front bodice

Attaching the side panels to the inserts

With right sides together, pin and stitch a center front panel to one long edge of an insert (diag 2).

Diag 2

Trim the seam and neaten the raw edge. Press the panel away from the insert. Attach a front side panel to the other long edge of the insert in the same manner (diag 3).

Repeat for the remaining front, ensuring you have a left and a right front. Topstitch each seam.

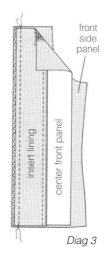

front side panel

insert lining

center front panel

Diag 3

Attaching the yokes

With right sides together, pin the corresponding front yoke to the upper edge of each front (diag 4).

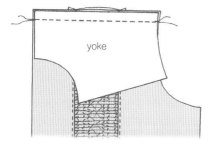

yoke

Diag 4

With the right side of the yoke lining facing the wrong side of the bodice, pin in place. The bodice is sandwiched between. Stitch *(diag 5)*.

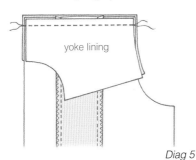

Diag 5

Trim the seam. Repeat for the remaining side.

Fold the front yoke away from the bodice and the lining towards the bodice. Topstitch the seam *(diag 6)*.

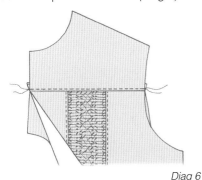

Diag 6

3. Buttonhole tabs

Fold the strip cut for the button tabs in half along the length and stitch using a ¼" (6mm) seam allowance *(diag 7)*.

Diag 7

Turn the strip through to the right side and press. Cut the strip into three lengths. With the seamed edge to the inside, fold the tabs in half with a triangle facing up. Topstitch around the outer edge *(diag 8)*.

Diag 8

4. Back bodice

Attaching the side panels

Clipping the curves on the center back panel and with right sides together, pin and stitch the corresponding back side panel to the sides of the center back panel *(diag 9)*. Trim the seams and neaten the raw edges. Press the seams towards the center back panel. Topstitch the seams.

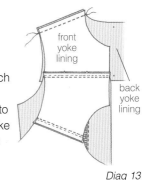

Diag 9

Attaching the yoke

Center one button tab, with the triangle facing up, on the upper edge of the back bodice and baste in place *(diag 10)*.

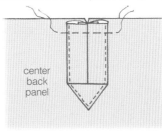

Diag 10

With right sides together and matching centers, pin and stitch the back yoke to the upper edge of the lower back panel *(diag 11)*. The tab is sandwiched between.

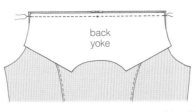

Diag 11

Trim the seam. Press towards the yoke.

5. Shoulder seams

With right sides together, pin and stitch the front yoke pieces to the back yoke at the shoulders *(diag 12)*.

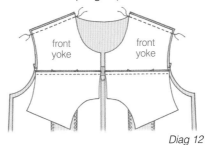

Diag 12

Trim the seams and press towards the back. Topstitch the seams.

Neaten the lower edge of the back yoke lining. Pin and stitch the back yoke lining to the front yoke lining at the shoulders *(diag 13)*.

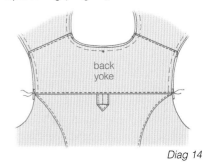

Diag 13

Trim the seams and press towards the front. With wrong sides together and matching seams and raw edges, position the yoke lining inside the yoke and pin in place. Tack. Topstitch the back yoke, catching the lining with the topstitching *(diag 14)*.

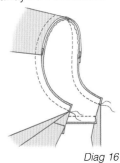

Diag 14

6. Sleeves

Stitch two rows of machine easing across the head of each sleeve at the positions indicated on the pattern. With right sides together, pin and stitch a sleeve band to the lower edge of each sleeve *(diag 15)*.

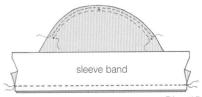

Diag 15

Press the band away from the sleeve.

Matching marks and easing the sleeve head to fit, pin each sleeve into the corresponding armhole. Stitch *(diag 16)*.

Diag 16

Trim the seam and neaten. Press towards the sleeve. Press under the seam allowance on the lower edge of the sleeve bands.

7. Side seams

With right sides together and matching sleeve seams, pin and stitch the front to the back at the sides, including the sleeve underarm seam (diag 17).

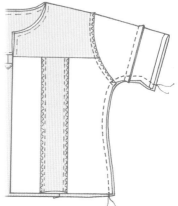

Diag 17

Trim the seams and neaten. Press the seams towards the back. Topstitch the side seam only.

Clip the seam halfway down the sleeve band and press the small section below the clip in the opposite direction (diag 18).

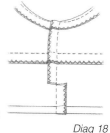

Diag 18

Fold half the band to the inside. Pin the fold to just cover the previous row of stitching. Tack in place. Topstitch the seam close to the folded edge (diag 19).

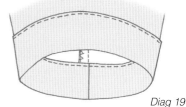

Diag 19

Topstitch the bodice side seams up to the sleeve seam only.

8. Skirt

With right sides together, stitch the two back skirt pieces together down the center back. Trim the seam and neaten. Press the seam to one side. Topstitch.

With right sides together, pin and stitch each front skirt piece to the back skirt at the sides (diag 20).

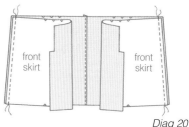

Diag 20

Trim the seams and neaten. Press towards the back and topstitch.

9. Pockets

Small pockets

Press under $\frac{3}{8}$" (1cm), then $\frac{5}{8}$" (1.5cm) at the top edge of the large and small pocket pieces. Machine stitch the hem close to the fold using the topstitch thread (diag 21).

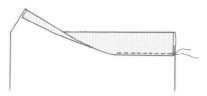

Diag 21

Attach an eyelet 1" (2.5cm) from the edges in both lower corners of the small pockets. Press under the seam allowance on the lower raw edge and then the sides.

Center the small pockets over the large pockets with the upper edges aligned and pin. Securing the ends, topstitch the small pockets in place (diag 22).

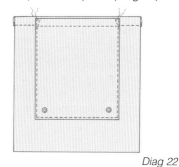

Diag 22

Pocket flaps

With the point of the triangle facing down, position one button tab in the center of one long raw edge of a pocket flap piece. Baste in place. With right sides together, stitch another flap piece

to the first around three sides, including the edge where the tab is sandwiched between (diag 23).

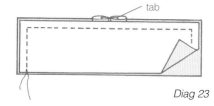

Diag 23

Trim the seam and clip the corners. Turn to the right side, carefully pushing out the corners. Press and topstitch the seamed sides.

Attaching the large pockets and flaps

Press under the seam allowance along the lower edge and then the sides of the pockets. Center a pocket on each skirt side seam, 4 $\frac{1}{8}$" (10.5cm) down from the top edge and pin. Securing the ends, topstitch the pockets in the same manner as the small pockets.

Pin a flap $\frac{5}{16}$" (8mm) above each pocket and stitch in place using a $\frac{1}{4}$" (6mm) seam allowance (diag 24).

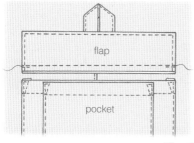

Diag 24

Trim the seam allowance and press the flap downwards. Securing the ends, topstitch (diag 25).

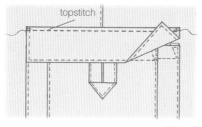

Diag 25

10. Attaching the skirt

Belt loops

Press under $\frac{1}{4}$" (6mm) on both long edges of the belt loop strip. Fold the strip in half along the length. Topstitch both long edges *(diag 26)*. Cut the strip into eight lengths. With the seams facing in the same direction, pin the raw end of a loop at each side of each smocked insert, at the side seams and the back side panel seams. Baste *(diag 27)*.

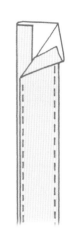

Diag 26

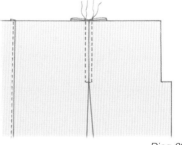

Diag 27

Skirt

Matching marks, fold the pleats right sides together and stitch down to the marked point. Fold into a box pleat and press. Topstitch both sides of the seam and across the lower end *(diag 28)*.

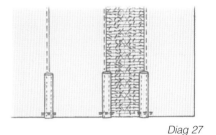

Diag 28

Matching center backs, side seams and the belt loops with the pleats at the back, pin and stitch the upper edge of the skirt to the lower edge of the hip band *(diag 29)*.

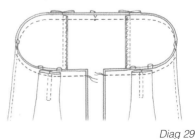

Diag 29

Hip facing

With right sides together, stitch a front facing to each side of the back facing *(diag 30)*.

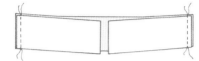

Diag 30

Press the seams open. Neaten the lower edge. Matching the stitching of the side seams and with the right side of the facing towards the wrong side of the bodice, pin and stitch the upper edge of the facing to the lower edge of the bodice *(diag 31)*.

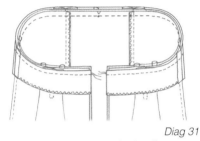

Diag 31

The belt loops and bodice are sandwiched between.

Trim the seam. Press the facing and skirt downwards. Topstitch the seam through all layers. Stitch again 1 ⅝" (4cm) below, securing the lower edge of the facing *(diag 32)*.

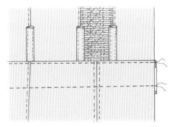

Diag 32

Fold under the raw edge at the lower end of the belt loops and stitch to secure ³⁄₁₆" (5mm) below the last row of stitching *(diag 33)*.

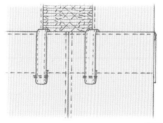

Diag 33

11. Front button bands

With right sides together, pin and stitch the center front seam in the skirt. Trim the seam and press to one side. Topstitch.

Staystitch around the lower edge of the opening, just inside the seam allowance. Clip almost up to the stitching in the corners *(diag 34)*.

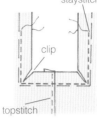

Diag 34

Fuse interfacing onto the wrong side of one half of each band. With right sides together, pin and stitch the long edge of the interfaced half of one button band to the right front opening edge, ending the seam at the clipped point *(diag 35)*.

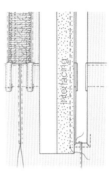

Diag 35

There will be ⅜" (1cm) of the band extending below this point. Press under ¼" (6mm) of this allowance then unfold. Press the band away from the front. Press under the seam allowance on the remaining long raw edge of the band. Fold half the band to the wrong side, aligning the fold with the previous line of stitching and tack in place. Topstitch the seam, ending ¾" (2cm) from the clipped point *(diag 36)*.

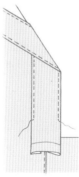

Diag 36

Topstitch the outer edge, ending level with the previous stitching.

Interface and attach the remaining band to the left front opening edge in a similar manner. This time, neaten the lower edge and leave the seam allowance extending.

Securing the lower end

Position the left band through the clipped point and behind the lower end of the opening *(diag 37)*. Pin the right band over the top aligning edges. Fold lower raw edge under. Topstitch a 1" (2.5cm) square around the end of the band and then diagonally across the corners of the square *(diag 38)*.

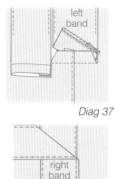

Diag 37

Diag 38

12. Collar

Fuse interfacing to the wrong side of one collar and one collar stand piece. With right sides together, stitch the collar pieces together around the outer edge *(diag 39)*.

Diag 39

Trim the seam, clip the corners and turn to the right side. Press. Topstitch the seam. Matching centers and marks, and with the uninterfaced side of the collar facing the stand, pin and baste the collar to the interfaced collar stand. Place the interfaced stand lining over the stand (the collar is sandwiched between). Pin and stitch *(diag 40)*.

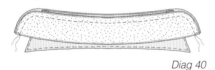

Diag 40

Trim the seam to ⅛" (2-3mm). With right sides together and matching centers and marks, pin and stitch the uninterfaced stand to the neckline *(diag 41)*.

Diag 41

Trim the seam, clip the curves and press towards the stand.

Press under the seam allowance on the lower raw edge of the stand lining and trim to ³⁄₁₆" (5mm). Turn the stand through to the right side and pin the folded edge to align with the neckline stitching on the wrong side. Tack in place. Topstitch around the collar stand *(diag 42)*.

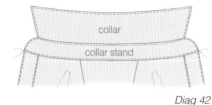

Diag 42

13. Belt

Fuse heavyweight interfacing to the wrong side of one belt piece. Pin the two belt pieces right sides together and stitch *(diag 43)*.

Diag 43

Trim the seam and clip the corners. Turn the belt through to the right side. Press. Neaten the raw end of the belt and topstitch 1 ³⁄₈" (3.5cm) from the edge on the remaining three sides. Work a ⅝" (1.5cm) horizontal buttonhole starting ¾" (2cm) from the neatened raw edge. Cut the buttonhole open. Place this end of the belt through the buckle, with the tongue in the buttonhole. Topstitch across the belt twice with the first line close to the neatening *(diag 44)*.

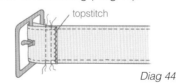

Diag 44

Center five eyelets 1" (2.5cm) apart at the end of the belt, with the first one 3" (7.5cm) from the end.

14. Finishing

Hem

Neaten the lower raw edge of the dress. Press under 1 ³⁄₈" (3cm). Machine stitch the hem using the topstitching thread. Press.

Buttons and buttonholes

With the first buttonhole aligned with the front yoke seam, stitch 7 vertical buttonholes evenly down the right front button band. Attach the buttons to correspond on the left band. Attach a button on each small pocket to correspond with the tab on the flap. Stitch a button on the back bodice to correspond with the tab extending from the back yoke.

For color photos and full details see pages 30 - 39

Sizes 1, 2, 3 and 4 years

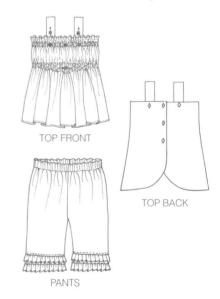

TOP FRONT

TOP BACK

PANTS

REQUIREMENTS

For full details, see page 32 and 34.

CUTTING OUT

See the liftout pattern sheet.

PREPARATION & PLEATING

For full instructions, see page 33.

SMOCKING & EMBROIDERY

For full instructions, see pages 33 - 39.

CONSTRUCTION

All seam allowances are ⅜" (1cm) unless otherwise specified.

TOP

1. Front hem

Turn under a ⅛" (2mm) hem twice on the lower edge of the front and machine stitch.

2. Side seams

Allowing ⅜" (1cm) of the back to extend past the upper and lower edges of the front, pin a corresponding back piece (right sides together) to each side of the front. Stitch (*diag 1*). Press the seam towards the back.

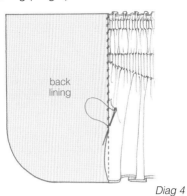

Diag 1

3. Back

Fuse a strip of interfacing onto the wrong side of the two remaining back sections in the area indicated on the pattern (*diag 2*). These will be the back lining pieces.

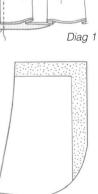

Diag 2

With right sides together, pin and stitch a corresponding lining piece to each back around three sides (*diag 3*).

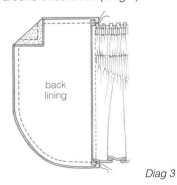

Diag 3

Trim the seam to ⅛" (2mm) and clip the corner. Turn to the right side and press. Press under the seam allowance along the side seam edges of the back lining and trim to ³⁄₁₆" (4mm). Pin and handstitch the fold to the side seam stitching (*diag 4*).

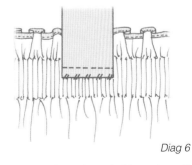

Diag 4

4. Shoulder straps

Cut out the embroidered straps. Fold each strap with right sides together and stitch along the long side and across the unembroidered end (*diag 5*).

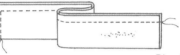

Diag 5

Trim the seam and clip the corners. Turn to the right side and press. Fold the raw edges on the remaining end to the inside and handstitch the opening closed.

With the embroidery facing out, center this end behind the side roses with the lower edge aligned with row 2 of the smocking. Securely handstitch each edge of each strap to the pleats. Then work a row of tiny running stitches ³⁄₁₆" (4mm) above the lower edge (*diag 6*).

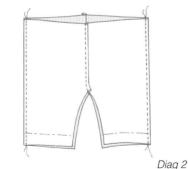

Diag 6

Take care that the stitching doesn't show on the right side.

5. Finishing

Stitch three buttonholes on the right back opening and two buttonholes on the upper edge, at the positions marked on the pattern. Using the instructions on page 35, attach the buttons on the left back opening to correspond with the buttonholes on the right back opening. Stitch the buttons in the center of the strap ends, adjusting the position to fit the child (*diag 7*).

Diag 7

The measurement on the diagram is given as a guide only.

CAPRI PANTS

1. Center front and back seams

Beginning with wrong sides together, stitch the two front pieces together at the center front using a French seam (*diag 1*).

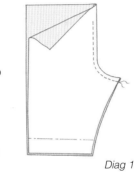

Diag 1

Clip the first line of stitching before enclosing it with the second line, forming the French seam. Press the seam to one side.

Repeat for the back pieces.

2. Side seams

Beginning with wrong sides together, stitch the front to the back at the sides using a French seam (*diag 2*). Press the seams towards the back.

Diag 2

Cut off a 2¼" (5.5cm) wide strip from the lower edge of both legs. Mark each one to ensure you can re-attach the correct strip to each leg in the next step.

3. Ruffles

Fold each ruffle strip in half and press. Baste the upper raw edges together. Using a ruffling attachment on your machine, ruffle the strip with tiny pleats approximately $5/16$" (8mm) apart. Alternatively, pin the pleats in position by hand and baste in place (diag 3).

Diag 3

Pin a ruffle to the lower edge of each leg and trim the excess (diag 4).

Diag 4

On the ends, ensure there isn't a pleat positioned close to the inside leg stitchline. Unpick if necessary.

Matching side seams, pin the strip to the lower leg edge, covering the ruffle. Stitch (diag 5).

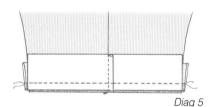

Diag 5

Trim and neaten the seam. Press towards the top edge. Topstitch the seam close to the fold (diag 6).

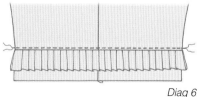

Diag 6

Attach a second ruffle to the lower edge of each leg in a similar manner.

4. Inside leg seams

With right sides together, matching center front and back seams and the ends of the ruffles, pin and stitch the inside leg seams. Trim and neaten the seam (diag 7). Press.

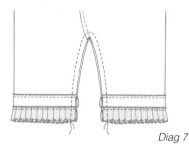

Diag 7

5. Elastic casing

Form the casing and insert the elastic following the general instructions on page 93.

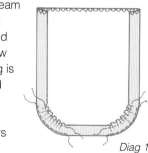

Shabby Chic

For color photos and full details see pages 40 - 45

Sizes 8, 10 and 12 years

TOP FRONT

TOP BACK

PANTS

REQUIREMENTS

For full details, see page 42 and 44.

CUTTING OUT

See the liftout pattern sheet.

PREPARATION & PLEATING

For full instructions, see page 43.

SMOCKING & EMBROIDERY

For full instructions, see pages 43 - 45.

CONSTRUCTION

All seam allowances are $3/8$" (1cm) unless otherwise specified.

TOP

1. Pocket

Neaten the top raw edge of the pocket with a machine zigzag or overlock stitch. Machine stitch two easing rows around the curves, one on the stitchline and the other, $1/8$" (3mm) from the raw edge. Pull up the second easing row until the seam allowance lies flat and the first row of stitching is on the fold (diag 1). Distribute the gathers evenly.

Diag 1

Press under the seam allowance on the sides and press the curved lower edge. Remove the easing thread from around the fold.

With right sides facing, place the smocked frill over the pocket, aligning the neatened edge of the pocket with the upper row of backsmocking. Pin in place, adjusting the frill until the stripes match the pocket and there is an even amount of flat fabric on the sides of the frill. Handstitch the neatened edge of the pocket to the backsmocking (diag 2).

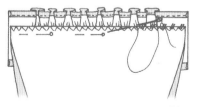

Diag 2

Press under the seam allowance on the ends of the frill and trim any excess.

With right sides facing, pin the pocket in place at the marked position on the left front. Securing the ends, stitch along the fold (diag 3).

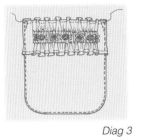

Diag 3

2. Shoulder seams

With right sides together and matching raw edges, stitch the front pieces to the back at the shoulders (diag 4).

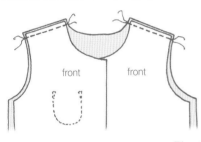

Diag 4

Trim and neaten the seams. Press towards the back.

3. Collar

Fuse interfacing onto the wrong side of the striped collar piece. This will be the upper collar.

With right sides together and matching raw edges, pin and stitch the upper collar to the print fabric undercollar (diag 5).

Diag 5

Trim the seam, clip the corners and turn to the right side. Press.

Clip the seam allowance up to the marked shoulder seam points on the neckline edge of the upper collar only.

Matching raw edges, center back marks and shoulder seams to collar markings, pin the collar to the neckline. The collar is pinned to the neckline along the back edge through the undercollar layer only. Ensure the upper collar is out of the way on this edge. Baste (diag 6).

Diag 6

Fuse interfacing to the wrong side of the front facings. Neaten the inner raw edges with a zigzag or overlock stitch. Press under the seam allowance on the shoulder seam edge of each facing. Stitch ¼" (6mm) from the fold.

With right sides together and matching raw edges, pin the facings to the fronts. The ends of the collar are sandwiched between. Stitch the neckline, including the back neckline edge of the undercollar (diag 7).

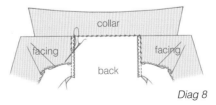

Diag 7

Trim the seam, clip the corners and curves. Turn the facings to the inside and press the front opening edges, including the front neckline sections. Clip the neckline seam at the marked shoulder point and press the back neck section towards the collar. Press under the seam allowance on the unsecured section of the upper collar. Trim to ¼" (6mm). Pin the fold to align with the collar stitching and handstitch in place. Handstitch the shoulder sections of the facing to the shoulder seams (diag 8).

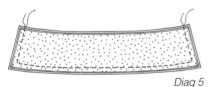

Diag 8

4. Setting in the sleeves

Stitch two easing rows across the head of each sleeve between the marks indicated on the pattern. Matching markings, pin the sleeves into the corresponding armhole. Pull up the easing to make the sleeve fit the armhole, ensuring no pleats are formed across the head of the sleeve. Stitch (diag 9).

Diag 9

Trim the seam and neaten. Press the seam towards the sleeve.

5. Lower facings

Unfold the front facings at the lower edge and turn to the outside. Baste across the lower edge. Neaten the upper edge of the lower facings with a machine zigzag or overlock stitch. With right sides together and matching raw edges, pin the facings to the lower edge. Stitch, securing the end of the seam at the marked point at the sides (diag 10).

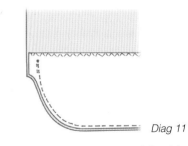

Diag 10

Trim the seam to ⅛" (3mm), ending ⅝" (1.5cm) below the ends of the stitching at the sides (diag 11).

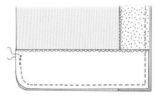

Diag 11

Clip the corners. Turn to the right side and press.

6. Lower sleeve and back facings

Attach the facings to the lower edge of the sleeves in a similar manner as the front (diag 12).

Diag 12

7. Side and sleeve seams

Neaten the raw edges of the sleeve and side seam edges on both sides of the top. With right sides together and matching underarm seams and raw edges, stitch from the lower edge of the top to the lower edge of the sleeve, securing the ends of the seam (diag 13).

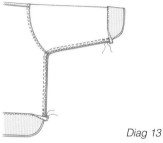

Diag 13

Ensure the ends of the facings are kept out of the way. Press the seam open. Press under the seam allowance on the side edges of each facing and handstitch this small section together (diag 14).

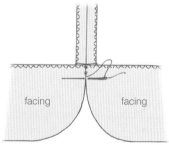

Diag 14

Tack the top edge of the facings in place and machine stitch close to the neatened edge around the lower edge of the top, continuing the stitching across the front opening facings (diag 15).

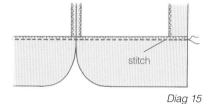

Diag 15

Repeat for the sleeves.

8. Finishing

Stitch the buttonholes at the marked positions on the left front opening. Attach the buttons on the right front opening to correspond.

Cut two 5 ½" (14cm) lengths of the narrow aqua ribbon and tie each piece

into a bow. Trim the ties diagonally. Attach a bow above each side opening (diag 16).

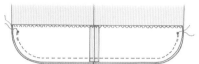

Diag 16

PANTS

1. Center front and back seams

Pin and stitch the two front pieces together at the center front (diag 1). Trim and neaten the seam. Press to one side. Repeat for the back pieces.

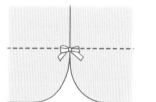

Diag 1

2. Inside leg seams

With right sides together and matching center front and back seams, stitch the front to the back along the inside leg (diag 2).

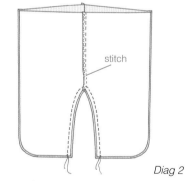

stitch

Diag 2

Trim and neaten the seam. Press towards the back.

3. Lower leg facings

With right sides together and matching raw edges, pin and stitch a front facing to each back facing on the inside leg (diag 3).

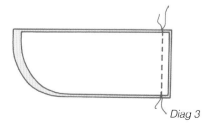

Diag 3

Press the seams open. Neaten the upper raw edge of each facing. Attach the facings in the same manner as the sleeves (diag 4).

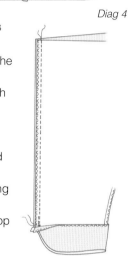

Diag 4

4. Side seams

Neaten each side edge on the front and back separately. With right sides together and matching raw edges, pin and stitch the side seams, securing the end of the seams at the top of the facing (diag 5). Keep the facings out of the way. Press the seams open.

Diag 5

Secure the upper edge of the facings in the same manner as the sleeves. Make two bows from the remaining length of narrow ribbon and attach in the same manner as before.

5. Elastic casing

Form the casing and insert the elastic following the general instructions on page 93.

Thread the wide aqua ribbon through the casing (using the buttonholes marked on the pattern). Trim the ends of the ribbon diagonally.

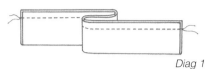

*For color photos and full details
see pages 46 - 51*

Sizes 4, 6, 8 and 10 years

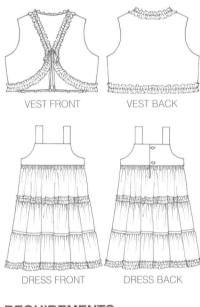

VEST FRONT   VEST BACK

DRESS FRONT   DRESS BACK

REQUIREMENTS

For full details, see page 48 and 50.

CUTTING OUT

See the liftout pattern sheet.

PREPARATION & PLEATING

For full instructions, see page 49.

SMOCKING & EMBROIDERY

For full instructions, see pages 49 - 51.

CONSTRUCTION

*All seam allowances are ³⁄₈" (1cm)
unless otherwise specified.*

DRESS

1. Shoulder straps

With right sides together and matching
raw edges, fold the straps in half down

the length. Stitch down the long side
(diag 1).

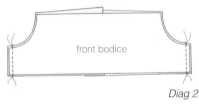

Diag 1

Trim the seam and turn to the right side.
Press, positioning the seam on one
edge.

2. Bodice

Fuse interfacing to the wrong side of the
back bodice lining pieces at the position
marked on the pattern. With right sides
together and matching raw edges,
stitch the front bodice to the back
bodice at the sides *(diag 2)*.

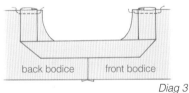

front bodice

Diag 2

Press the seams open. Repeat for the
bodice lining. With the seam towards
the armhole, pin one end of the straps to
the marked position on the upper edge
of the front bodice. Pin the other end of
the straps onto the corresponding
position on the back bodice. Baste
(diag 3).

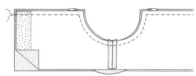

back bodice   front bodice

Diag 3

With right sides together and matching
raw edges, pin the bodice lining to the
bodice along the upper edge. Stitch
(diag 4).

Diag 4

Trim the seam. Clip the corners and
curves and turn through to the right
side. Press the upper edge. Press under
the seam allowance on the lower edge
of the lining and trim to ³⁄₁₆" (5mm).

3. Placket

*Note: Using a zipper foot allows you to
stitch as close as possible to the
beaded smocking.*

Staystitch
down both
sides of the
marked line at
the center
back, pivoting
at the lower
end *(diag 5)*. 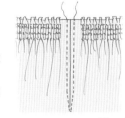 *Diag 5*

Cut down the marked line almost to the
stitching.

With right sides together and with the
staystitching on the stitchline of the
placket, stitch the placket to the
opening *(diag 6)*.

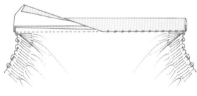

Diag 6

Press the placket away from the skirt.
Press under the seam allowance on the
remaining raw edge of the placket and
trim to ¼" (6mm). Fold the placket in half,
with the folded edge aligned with the
previous stitchline. Handstitch *(diag 7)*.

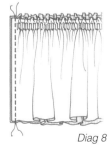

Diag 7

At the top edge, fold the right hand end
to the wrong side and baste. On the left,
the placket remains extended.

4. Skirt remaining side seam

The smocking does not require
blocking. Remove the pleating threads
except for the top holding row.

With right sides
together, pin
and stitch the
remaining side
seam *(diag 8)*.
Trim and neaten
the seam.
Press towards
the back. *Diag 8*

5. Assembling the skirt

Second tier. With right sides together, stitch the second tier pieces together to form a circle (diag 9).

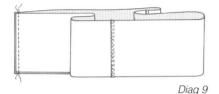

Diag 9

Trim the seams and neaten. Press to one side. Stitch two gathering rows along the top of the tier. Pull up the gathers to fit the lower edge of the first tier and adjust the gathers evenly. With right sides together, pin and stitch the second tier to the first tier (diag 10).

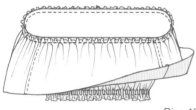

Diag 10

Trim the seam and neaten. Press towards the upper tier.

Join 4 voile strips into one length, pressing the seams open. Stitch two rows of machine gathering down the center of the strip. Pull up the gathers until the frill fits around the skirt on the previous seam, plus ¾" (2cm) excess. Adjust the gathers evenly. At one end fold ⅜" (1cm) of the frill under to hide the raw edge. Beginning at one side seam, ¼" (6mm) above the skirt seam, stitch down the center of the voile frill (diag 11).

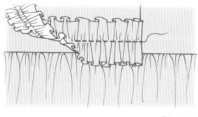

Diag 11

Attach the frill around the skirt, folding under the ⅜" (1cm) excess when you reach the beginning.

Third tier. Stitch the pieces together and attach this tier to the lower edge of the second tier in the same manner, omitting the voile frill.

Fold under the raw end of the length of satin ribbon. With the folded end at one seam and the lower edge of the ribbon aligned with the skirt seam, stitch the ribbon to the skirt along the upper and lower edges (diag 12).

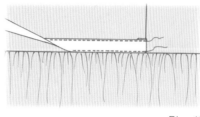

Diag 12

Fold under the raw end of the ribbon when you reach the beginning and trim the excess.

Neaten the lower raw edge of the tier. Press under ⅝" (1.5cm) and machine stitch the hem in place.

Join 8 ½ strips of voile into one length, gather the frill and attach it to the hem in the same manner as the first tier.

6. Attaching the skirt to the bodice

With right sides together, matching side seams and with the stitchline just above the first row of smocking, pin the lower edge of the bodice to the upper edge of the skirt. The bodice extends ⅜" (1cm) past the edges of the placket at the back. Stitch (diag 13).

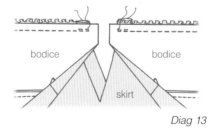

Diag 13

Trim the seam and press towards the bodice. Press under the seam allowance of the lower edge of the lining and trim to ³⁄₁₆" (5mm). Unfold at the center back. With right sides together and matching raw edges, pin and stitch down the center back on both sides of the back opening (diag 14).

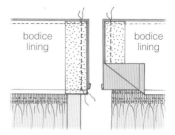

Diag 14

Trim the seam and clip the corner. Turn through to the right side and press.

Matching side seams, refold the lower edge of the lining and position to align with the bodice stitching. Handstitch (diag 15).

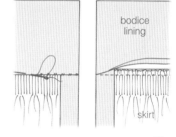

Diag 15

7. Finishing

Stitch the buttonholes on the right back bodice at the positions indicated on the pattern. Attach the buttons on the left back to correspond.

VEST

1. Shoulder seams

With right sides together, pin and stitch the two front pieces to the back at the shoulders (diag 1).

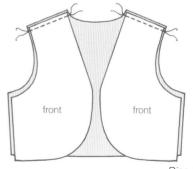

Diag 1

Press the seams open. Embellish the embroidered motifs on the fabric using the beads and sequins following the instructions on page 50. Ensure you do not attach the beads too close to the stitchlines as they may get in the way when stitching seams.

Stitch the shoulder seams on the vest lining in the same manner.

2. Attaching the lining

Cut two 14 ½" (37cm) lengths of satin ribbon. Position one end of each piece at the marked position on the front opening of the vest and baste *(diag 2)*.

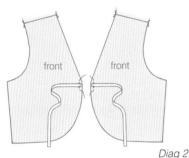

Diag 2

With right sides together, and matching raw edges, centers and seams, pin and stitch the lining to the vest around the outer edge, excluding the side seams *(diag 3)*.

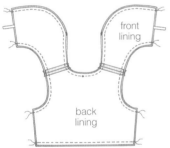

Diag 3

Ensure the ribbon ties are not caught in the stitching, except where they are basted to the front.

Trim the seams and clip the curves.

Turn the vest through to the right side by taking the fronts through to the back in the openings at the shoulder and then out through one of the side openings *(diag 4)*.

Diag 4

Roll the seams between your fingers to bring them to the edge and press.

3. Side seams

Matching seams and raw edges, pin and stitch the side seams, leaving an 3 ⅛" (8cm) opening in the lining sections *(diag 5)*.

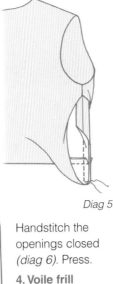

Diag 5

Handstitch the openings closed *(diag 6)*. Press.

4. Voile frill

Join 3 voile strips into one length, gather and attach the frill ⁵⁄₁₆" (8mm) away from the

Diag 6

edge around the outer edge of the vest in the same manner as the skirt frills *(diag 7)*.

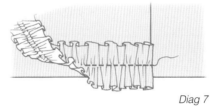

Diag 7

5. Finishing

Place a white glass bead onto the end of each ribbon tie. Push it along the ribbon and tie a knot ¾" (2cm) up from the end. Cut the end of the ties diagonally.

First Love

For color photos and full details see pages 52 - 57

Sizes 10, 12 and 14 years

FRONT   BACK

REQUIREMENTS

For full details, see page 54 and 55.

CUTTING OUT

See the liftout pattern sheet.

PREPARATION & PLEATING

For full instructions, see page 55.

SMOCKING

For full instructions, see page 55 and 56.

CONSTRUCTION

All seam allowances are ⅜" (1cm) unless otherwise specified.

1. Blocking and shaping the smocking

Remove the pleating threads, except for the upper holding row. Block the smocking following the general instructions, keeping it to the original tied-off measurement.

2. Shoulder seams

With right sides together, stitch the front bodice pieces to the back bodice at the shoulders *(diag 1)*.

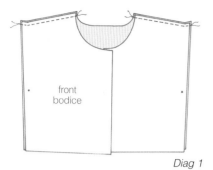

Diag 1

Trim and neaten the seams. Press towards the back.

3. Side seams

Neaten the raw edge along the sides and armhole edges. With right sides together and using a ⅝" (1.5cm) seam allowance, stitch the front bodice pieces to the back bodice up to the marked point at the sides *(diag 2)*. Secure the ends of the stitching.

Diag 2

Press the seam open and a ⅝" (1.5cm) hem allowance around the armholes. Using a short straight stitch, machine stitch the seam allowance close to the neatened edge around the armholes *(diag 3)*. Press.

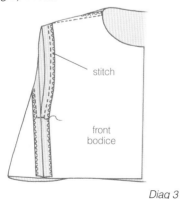

Diag 3

4. Front opening

Neaten the raw edge on both sides of the front opening. Press under a ¾" (2cm) facing on both edges. Stitch *(diag 4)*.

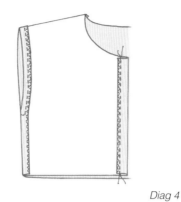

Diag 4

5. Binding the neckline

With ⅜" (1cm) extending at both ends and stretching the binding to fit, pin the binding around the neckline. Stitch *(diag 5)*.

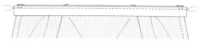

Diag 5

Press under the seam allowance on the remaining long edge of the binding. Fold the extending ends under and fold the binding to the inside. Align the folded edge to just cover the previous stitchline *(diag 6)*. Stretching the edge of the binding to fit, pin and tack in place. On the right side, stitch 'in the ditch' of the seam *(diag 7)*.

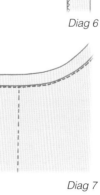

Diag 6

Diag 7

Handstitch the openings closed at the ends of the binding. Press the neckline.

6. Shirring the back skirt

Using a fabric marker and with the first line ½" (13mm) down from the top raw edge, rule five lines ½" (13mm) apart across the top of the back skirt. Mark the center of the skirt at the top edge.

Leaving a 2" (5cm) tail, secure the end of the shirring elastic just inside the seam allowance at one end of the first line. Stitch over the elastic with a mid-width zigzag stitch *(diag 8)*.

Diag 8

Pull the elastic gently and ensure it is not caught in the stitching. At the remaining end, trim the elastic, leaving a 4" (10cm) tail. Wind this tail around a safety pin to ensure it doesn't slip back into the stitching.

Stitch elastic along the remaining four lines in the same manner.

Unwind the elastic tails from the safety pins and pull on them (as you would gathering threads) to gather the shirred panel evenly until it measures the following in width excluding seam allowances

Size 10: 10 ¼" (26cm)

Size 12: 11" (28cm)

Size 14: 11 ¾" (30cm)

Secure the ends of the elastic in the same manner as the other side and trim the tails.

7. Skirt side seams

Using a ⅝" (1.5cm) seam allowance and aligning the upper shirring row with the first backsmocked row, stitch the front skirt to the back skirt at the sides. Stitch to within 4 ¾" (12cm) of the lower edge, securing the end of the stitching *(diag 9)*.

Diag 9

Neaten both edges of the seams separately and press open.

8. Attaching the skirt to the bodice

Cross the right front opening over the left at the lower end by ⅜" (1cm) and baste in place *(diag 10)*.

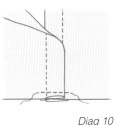

Diag 10

With right sides together and matching side seams and centers, pin the skirt to the lower edge of the bodice *(diag 11)*.

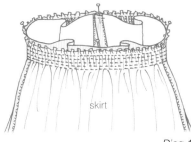

skirt

Diag 11

The upper edge of the skirt will be smaller than the lower edge of the bodice. Stretching the skirt to fit the bodice, stitch together using a short straight stitch or an appropriate straight stretch stitch on your machine *(diag 12)*.

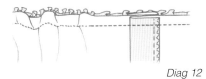

Diag 12

Trim the seam and neaten.

9. Hem and side splits

Open out the seam allowance at the lower ends of the side splits. Neaten the lower raw edges of the skirt.

Press under a 1" (2.5cm) hem on both sections of the skirt. Refold the hems on the splits and topstitch ⅜" (1cm) from the fold, pivoting to turn the corners at the top of the splits.

Machine stitch the hems in place ¾" (2cm) from the lower edge using the twin-needle *(diag 13)*. Press the hem and side splits.

Diag 13

10. Finishing

Work a thread loop on the left hand end of the neck binding. Ensuring the stitching doesn't show on the right side, attach a button on the other end of the binding on the inside *(diag 14)*.

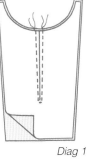

Diag 14

Work another thread loop and attach a button on the inside of the front opening half way down the opening.

For color photos and full details see pages 58 - 63

Sizes newborn, 3, 6 and 12 months

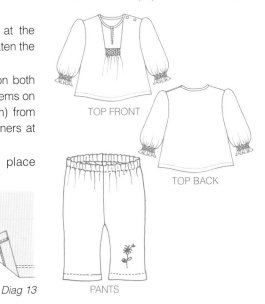

TOP FRONT

TOP BACK

PANTS

REQUIREMENTS

For full details, see page 60 and 61.

CUTTING OUT

See the liftout pattern sheet.

PREPARATION & PLEATING

For full instructions, see page 61.

SMOCKING & EMBROIDERY

For full instructions, see pages 61 - 63.

CONSTRUCTION

All seam allowances are ⅜" (1cm) unless otherwise specified.

TOP

1. Front insert

Place the front insert pieces with right sides together. Stitch down one side of the line marking the front opening, pivot and place one stitch across the end. Pivot and stitch up the remaining side of the opening *(diag 1)*.

Diag 1

Cut down the marked line almost up to the stitching. Turn through to the right side and topstitch the opening close to the fold *(diag 2)*.

Diag 2

Press and tack the layers together around the outer edge.

Staystitch the corners above the smocking and clip the corners almost up to the stitching *(diag 3)*.

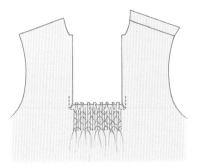

Diag 3

With right sides together and matching raw edges, pin and stitch the front insert to the front opening *(diag 4)*.

Trim the seam and neaten with a machine zigzag or overlock stitch.

Press the seam away from the insert.

Diag 4

2. Right shoulder seam

With right sides together, stitch the front to the back at the right shoulder *(diag 5)*.

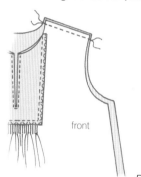

Diag 5

Trim and neaten the seam and press towards the back.

3. Binding the neckline

Left front neck. Neaten the raw edge on the left shoulder. Press under ¾" (2cm). Fold the left neck binding in half. With right sides together and ¼" (6mm) extending at both ends, pin the binding to the neckline. Trim any excess binding. Stitch *(diag 6)*.

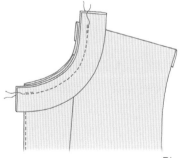

Diag 6

Trim the seam to ⁵⁄₁₆" (7mm). Fold under the extending ends and fold the binding over the seam, aligning the fold with the previous stitchline. Handstitch *(diag 7)*.

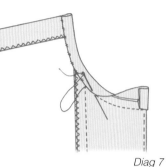

Diag 7

Right front and back neckline.

Attach the remaining binding to the neckline in a similar manner as the left front neckline with the following exception. Leave a raw edge on the end of the binding at the left back shoulder *(diag 8)*.

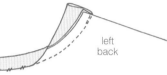

Diag 8

4. Back left shoulder

With the right side of the tab facing the wrong side of the back, and with ¼" (6mm) extending past the neck binding, stitch the tab to the back left shoulder *(diag 9)*.

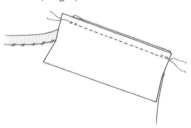

Diag 9

Press under ¼" (6mm) on the remaining long edge of the tab. Fold the tab right sides together and stitch across the neck edge *(diag 10)*.

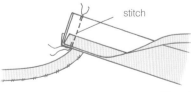

Diag 10

Turn through to the right side and position the fold of the tab to just cover the stitchline. Topstitch to secure the tab *(diag 11)*.

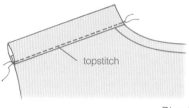

Diag 11

Matching raw edges, place the left front shoulder over the back left shoulder at the armhole edge and baste *(diag 12)*.

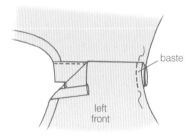

Diag 12

5. Setting in the sleeves

Stitch two rows of machine gathering across the head of the sleeves between the marks indicated on the pattern.

Matching raw edges and marks, pin a sleeve into each armhole, pulling up the gathers to fit. Stitch *(diag 13)*.

Diag 13

Trim the seams and neaten. Press towards the sleeve.

6. Side seams

With right sides together and matching sleeve seams and the smocking rows, pin and stitch the front to the back including the underarm seam *(diag 14)*.

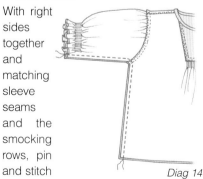

Diag 14

Trim and neaten the seams. Press towards the back.

7. Hem

Neaten the lower raw edge. Press under ¾" (2cm) and using a stretch stitch or tiny zigzag, machine stitch the hem in place.

8. Finishing

Attach the two popper studs on the left shoulder opening, following the manufacturer's instructions.

Work a thread loop on the end of the right front neck binding (diag 15).

Diag 15

Attach a button on the left front binding to correspond. The ends of the binding do not overlap.

PANTS

1. Center front and back seams

With right sides together, pin and stitch the two front pieces together at the center front using a very short straight stitch or tiny zigzag (diag 1).

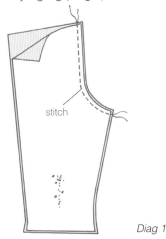

Diag 1

Trim and neaten the seams. Press to one side.

Repeat for the back pieces.

2. Side seams

With right sides together, stitch the front to the back at the sides. Trim and neaten the seams. At the lower edge, clip the seam at the hem foldline. Press the upper section of the seams towards the back and the small section at the lower end towards the front.

3. Inside leg seams

Matching center front and back seams, pin and stitch the inside leg seams (diag 2).

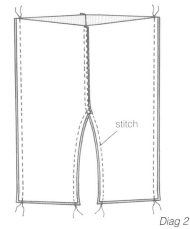

stitch

Diag 2

Trim and neaten the seam. Press towards the back.

4. Elastic casing

Neaten the upper raw edge. Press under 1 ¼" (3cm). Stitch the casing in place, insert the elastic and finish the casing following the general instructions on page 93.

5. Hem

Neaten the lower edge of each leg. Press under the hem allowance. Machine stitch the hems using a short, narrow zigzag stitch or stretch stitch (diag 3).

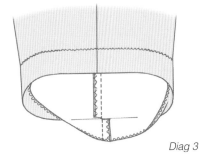

Diag 3

For color photos and full details see pages 64 - 71

Skirt sizes 8, 10, 12 and 14 years

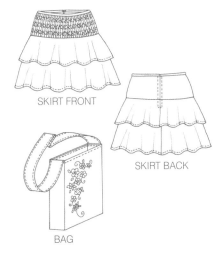

SKIRT FRONT

SKIRT BACK

BAG

REQUIREMENTS

For full details, see pages 66, 68, 70 and 71.

CUTTING OUT

See the liftout pattern sheet.

PLEATING

For full instructions, see page 66.

SMOCKING & EMBROIDERY

For full instructions, see pages 67 - 70.

CONSTRUCTION

All seam allowances are ⅜" (1cm) unless otherwise specified.

SKIRT

1. Blocking and shaping the smocking

Block the panel to fit the front yoke lining, following the general instructions on page 93.

Remove the pleating threads.

Matching the upper stitchline half way between the upper holding rows and the lower stitchline aligned with the first of the lower holding rows, fuse the yoke interfacing to the back of the smocked panel *(diag 1)*.

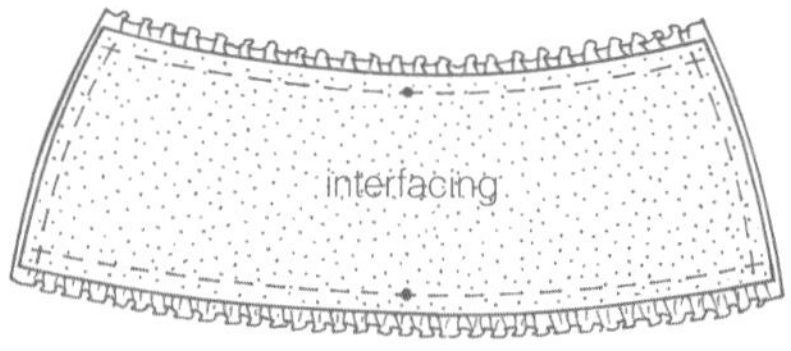

Diag 1

Adjust the smocking to fit the curves of the interfacing. Trim off the excess fabric from the smocked panel.

2. Forming the skirt yoke and yoke lining

Fuse interfacing to the wrong side of two back yoke pieces. With right sides together, pin and stitch an interfaced back yoke piece to each side of the smocked front yoke *(diag 2)*.

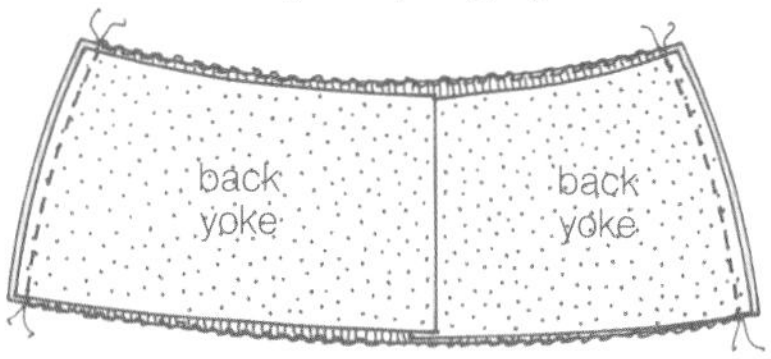

Diag 2

Trim the seams and press towards the back.

Repeat for the lining pieces, pressing the seams open.

With wrong sides together and matching raw edges and side seams, place the yoke lining behind the yoke and baste together around the outer edges within the seam allowance *(diag 3)*.

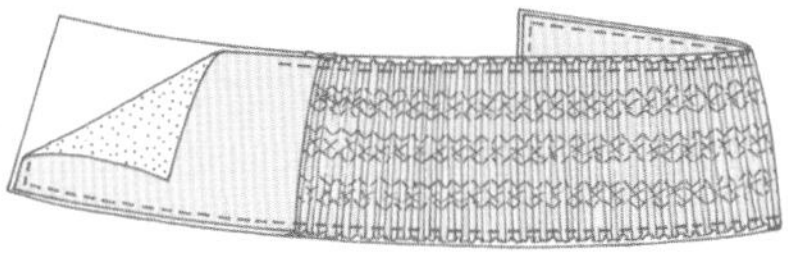

Diag 3

Neaten both sides of the center back opening.

3. Skirt

Neaten the center back edges of the upper back skirt pieces. Repeat on the back underskirt pieces. With right sides together, pin and stitch an upper back skirt piece to each side of the upper front skirt *(diag 4)*.

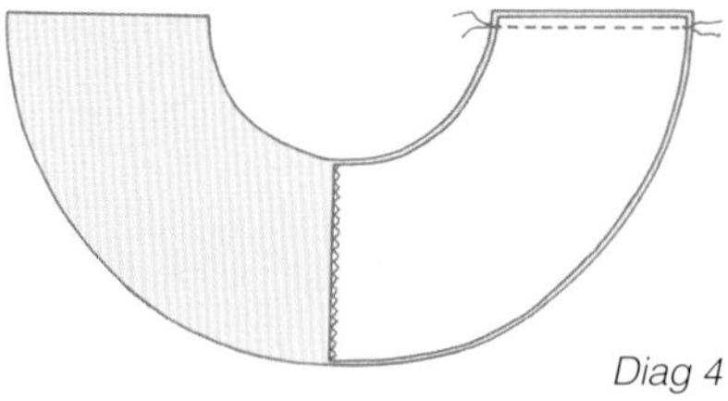

Diag 4

Trim and neaten the seams and press towards the back.

Stitch the side seams of the underskirt in the same manner as the upper skirt.

Matching side seams and raw edges, and placing the right side of the underskirt to the wrong side of the upper skirt, pin the two sections together and baste along the upper edge *(diag 5)*.

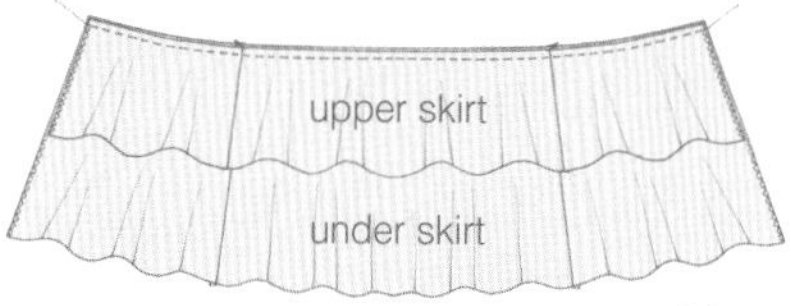

Diag 5

4. Attaching the skirt

With right sides together and matching raw edges and side seams, pin and stitch the skirt to the lower edge of the yoke *(diag 6)*.

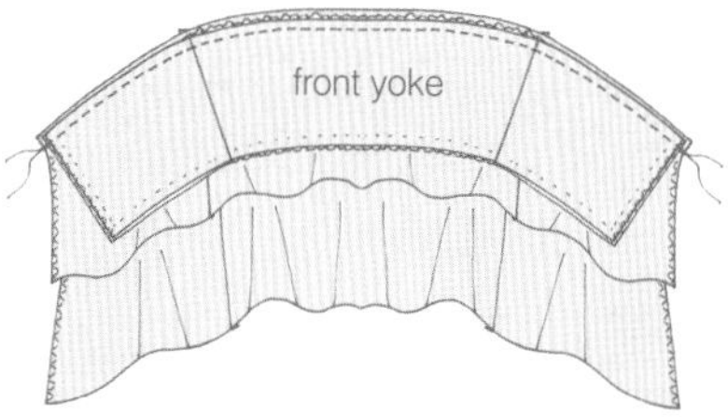

Diag 6

Trim and neaten the seam. Press towards the skirt.

5. Center back seams

With right sides together and matching raw edges, stitch the center back seam of the upper skirt up to the marked point, using a ⅝" (1.5cm) seam allowance *(diag 7)*.

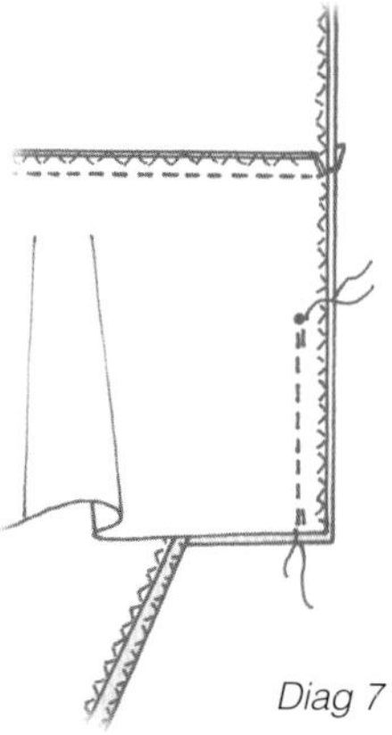

Diag 7

Ensure the underskirt pieces are kept out of the way. Press the seam open.

Clip the seam allowance on the upper skirt up to the stitching at the end of the opening for the zipper *(diag 8)*.

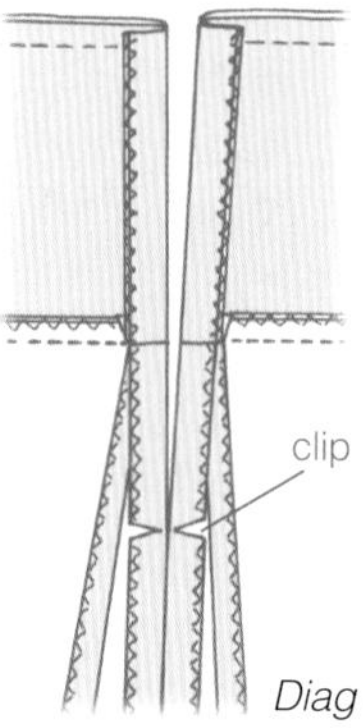

Diag 8

Stitch the underskirt center back seam in the same manner, omitting the clipping.

Fold the two sides of the upper skirt opening over the underskirt to the inside. Press. Tack the seam allowances together along the sides of the opening *(diag 9)*.

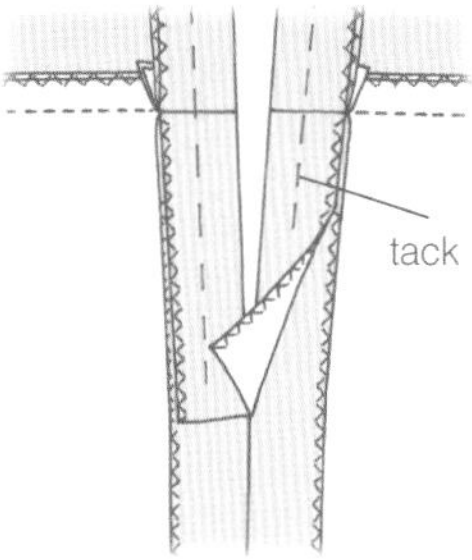

Diag 9

6. Inserting the zipper

Center the zipper under the opening. Pin and tack in place. Stitch ¼" (6mm) away from the zipper and across the end *(diag 10)*.

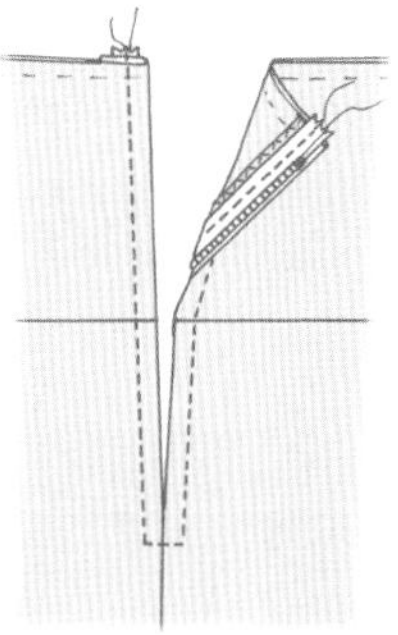

Diag 10

7. Binding the waistline

Fold the binding in half along the length and press. Matching raw edges, pin the binding to the upper edge on the inside, allowing ⅜" (1cm) to extend at both ends. Stitch *(diag 11)*.

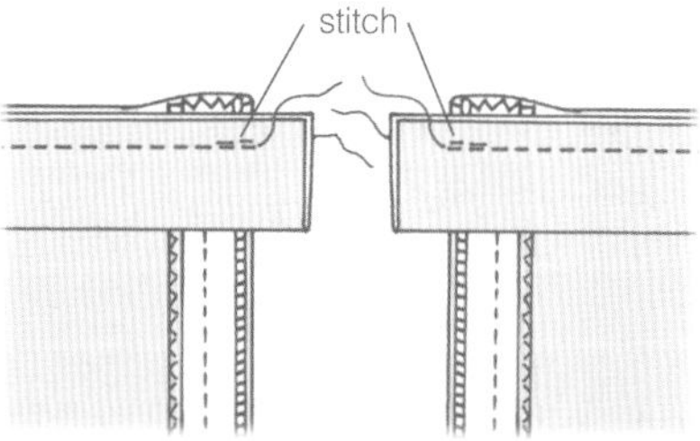

Diag 11

Fold in the ends of the binding and wrap the binding over the seam to the right side. Pin and tack in place, ensuring the fold of the binding extends over the stitchline on the right side. On the right side, topstitch along the edge of the binding close to the folded edge (diag 12).

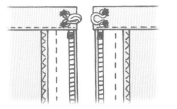

Diag 12

Handstitch the ends of the binding to secure.

8. Finishing

Neaten the lower edge of the upper skirt with an overlock or zigzag stitch. Press under a ¼" (6mm) hem and machine stitch in place. Repeat for the underskirt.

On the inside, stitch the hook and eye in place on the ends of the waist binding (diag 13).

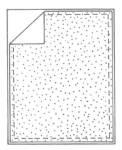

Diag 13

BAG

1. Interfacing the bag

Pin a piece of interfacing on the wrong side of the front and tack along all sides (diag 1).

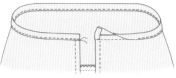

Diag 1

Repeat for the back, and the side and base piece.

2. Forming the bag

Mark the center of the bag front on the lower edge. Fold the side and base piece in half and mark the center on both long edges of the strip. Matching the center marks first, pin the strip around the front, clipping the seam allowance to ease it around the corners. Stitch (diag 2).

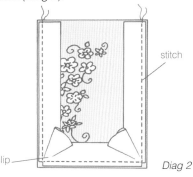

Diag 2

Trim the seam and press away from the front. Attach the back to the remaining long edge of the strip in the same manner. Turn the bag to the right side.

3. Bag lining

Construct the lining in the same manner as the bag, leaving the lining with the wrong side facing outwards.

4. Strap

Tack interfacing to the wrong side of the strap in the same manner as the bag. Press under ⅜" (1cm) on both long sides of the strap. Fold the strap in half along the length, wrong sides together. Tack in place.

Stitch along both sides of the strap ⅛" (2-3mm) from the folded edge (diag 3).

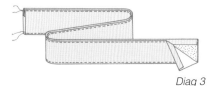

Diag 3

5. Attaching the strap and lining

Press under ⅜" (1cm) along the top edge of the bag. Press under ⅝" (1.5cm) along the top edge of the lining.

Pin the ends of the strap inside the bag, aligning the sides of the strap with the side seams of the bag (diag 4).

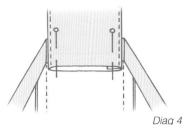

Diag 4

Place the lining inside the bag, matching seams and aligning the folded edges of the lining ³⁄₁₆" (5mm) below the bag. Pin and tack in place.

Stitch around the upper edge of the bag ⅜" (1cm) away from the fold, ensuring the thread in the bobbin matches the lining fabric (diag 5).

Diag 5

For color photos and full details see pages 72 - 77

Sizes 6, 12 and 24 months

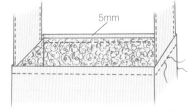

TOP FRONT   TOP BACK

PANTS FRONT   PANTS BACK

REQUIREMENTS

For full details, see page 74 and 76.

CUTTING OUT

See the liftout pattern sheet.

PREPARATION & PLEATING

For full instructions, see page 75.

SMOCKING & EMBROIDERY

For full instructions, see pages 75 - 77.

CONSTRUCTION

All seam allowances are ⅜" (1cm) unless otherwise specified.

TOP

1. Blocking and shaping the smocking

Block the smocking following the instructions on page 93, leaving the upper holding row in place. Work the embroidery following the instructions on pages 76 and 77. Position the blocking guide over the panel, matching centers and aligning the lower stitchline with the lowest row of smocking. Mark the neckline and armhole shaping (diag 1).

Diag 1

Using a short straight stitch or narrow zigzag, stitch just inside the marked neckline to secure the smocking. Cut out along the marked lines.

2. Lining

Fold under a double ³⁄₁₆" (5mm) hem and press. Stitch close to the folded edge (diag 2).

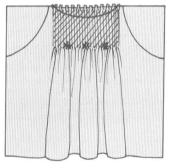

front lining

Diag 2

With wrong sides together and matching neckline and armhole edges,

pin the lining to the smocked front and baste within the seam allowance (diag 3).

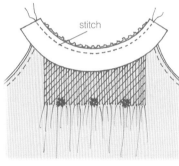

baste

Diag 3

3. Binding the neckline

With right sides together and matching raw edges and centers, pin the binding to the neckline. Stitch (diag 4).

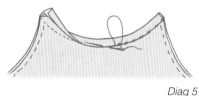

stitch

Diag 4

Fold under ³⁄₁₆" (5mm) on the remaining raw edge, then fold the binding to the wrong side and pin, aligning the folded edge with the previous stitchline. Handstitch in place (diag 5).

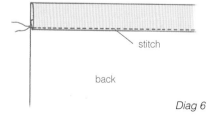

Diag 5

4. Elastic casing for the back

Fold under ³⁄₁₆" (5mm) along the upper edge of the back piece and press. Press under a further ½" (13mm) and press. Stitch close to the folded edge to form a casing (diag 6).

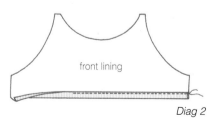

stitch

back

Diag 6

Cut a 6 ⅜" (16cm) length of the non roll elastic. Thread the elastic through the casing and stitch to secure at both ends of the casing (diag 7).

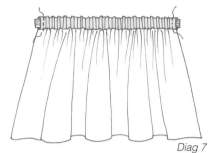

Diag 7

5. Side seams

With right sides together and matching raw edges, pin and stitch the front to the back at the sides (diag 8). Trim and neaten the seams. Press towards the front.

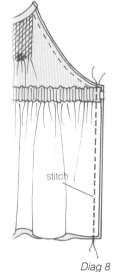

stitch

Diag 8

6. Pocket

Fold under ³⁄₁₆" (5mm) on the upper edge of the pocket and press.

Fold under a further ⅝" (15mm) and press. Topstitch in place with the red thread ⅜" (1cm) from the folded edge (diag 9).

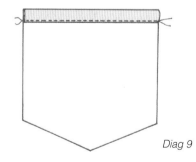

Diag 9

Embroider the daisy and leaves at the marked position. Press under the seam allowance at the sides and then the lower edges. Aligning the side of the pocket 4 ½" (11.5cm) from the right hand side seam and the point 1 ⅜" (3.5cm) above the lower raw edge, pin the pocket to the top. Beginning and ending securely, topstitch the pocket in place close to the folded edges *(diag 10)*.

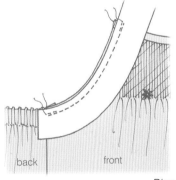

Diag 10

7. Straps and armhole binding

With ³⁄₈" (1cm) of the binding extending past the side seam and the remainder extending at the neckline, pin and stitch a length of binding to each side of the bodice *(diag 11)*.

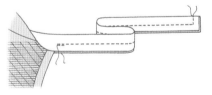

Diag 11

Fold the extending binding in half, right sides together at the neckline. Stitch along the binding and across the narrow end *(diag 12)*.

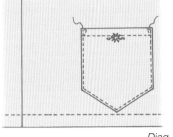

Diag 12

Trim the seam, clip the corners and turn the tie to the right side.

Press under the seam allowance on the unsecured section. Fold under the end of the binding at the side seam.

Fold the binding to the wrong side aligning the folded edge with the previous stitchline and pin. Handstitch in place *(diag 13)*. Press.

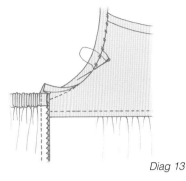

Diag 13

Repeat for the remaining strap and armhole binding piece.

8. Hem

Fold under ³⁄₈" (1cm) on the lower edge and press. Fold under a further ³⁄₈" (1cm) and press. Using matching machine thread in the bobbin only, topstitch the hem in place using the red topstitching thread and a slightly longer stitch length than usual (approx. ⅛" or 3mm).

PANTS

All seam allowances are ³⁄₈" (1cm) unless otherwise specified.

1. Front and back seams

With right sides together and matching raw edges, pin the front pieces down the center. Stitch *(diag 1)*.

Trim and neaten the seam. Press to one side. Repeat for the back.

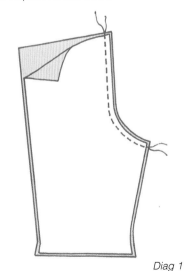

Diag 1

2. Side seams

With right sides together and matching raw edges, pin and stitch the front to the back at the sides *(diag 2)*.

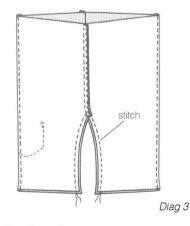

Diag 2

Trim and neaten the seams. Clip the seam ³⁄₄" (2cm) from the lower edge. Press the upper section towards the back and the lower section towards the front.

3. Pocket

Construct the pocket in the same manner as the top. Pin and topstitch the pocket in place at the marked position on the left leg.

4. Inside leg

With right sides together and matching raw edges and center seams, pin the front to the back along the inside legs. Stitch *(diag 3)*. Trim and neaten the seam.

Diag 3

5. Elastic casing

Form the casing and insert the elastic following the general instructions on page 93.

6. Hems

Press under ³⁄₈" (1cm) on the lower edge of each leg. Press under a further ³⁄₈" (1cm). Topstitch close to the folded edge.